B
2430
T374
K57

85-04304

ROESCH LIBRARY
UNIVERSITY OF DAYTON
DAYTON, OHIO 45469

ASPECTS OF THE THOUGHT
OF
TEILHARD DE CHARDIN

ASPECTS OF THE THOUGHT OF TEILHARD DE CHARDIN

By

FRANCIS J. KLAUDER, S.D.B., Ph.D.

THE CHRISTOPHER PUBLISHING HOUSE
NORTH QUINCY, MASSACHUSETTS

COPYRIGHT © 1971
BY FRANCIS J. KLAUDER
Library of Congress Catalog Card Number 70-155359
SBN: 8158-0259-5

Nihil Obstat: Joseph M. Occhio, S.D.B., S.T.L., Ph.D.
              Censor Librorum
              January 1, 1971

Imprimi Potest: John J. Malloy, S.D.B., S.T.L., M.A.
                Provincial

† Imprimatur: Lawrence B. Casey, D.D.
             Bishop of Paterson
             January 31, 1971

PRINTED IN THE UNITED STATES OF AMERICA

**TRIUMPHANTI
SPIRITUI
SANCTO**

ACKNOWLEDGMENTS

The author wishes to acknowledge the following books which he has made reference to, from time to time, in compiling and writing the contents of his study of the thought of Teilhard de Chardin.

The Appearance of Man by Pierre Teilhard de Chardin. Copyright 1956 by Editions du Seuil. Copyright 1965 in the English translation by William Collins Sons & Co., Ltd., London, and Harper & Row, Publishers, Inc., New York.

Building the Earth by Pierre Teilhard de Chardin. Published by Dimension Books, Wilkes-Barre, Pa., 1965.

The Divine Milieu by Pierre Teilhard de Chardin. Copyright 1957 by Editions du Seuil, Paris. English translation copyright 1960 by William Collins Sons & Co., Ltd., London, and Harper & Row, Publishers, Inc., New York.

The Future of Man by Pierre Teilhard de Chardin. Translated from the French by Norman Denny. Copyright 1959 by Editions du Seuil, Paris. Copyright 1964 in the English translation by William Collins Sons & Co., Ltd., London, and Harper & Row, Publishers, Inc., New York.

Hymn of the Universe by Pierre Teilhard de Chardin. Copyright 1965 by Harper & Row, New York.

Letters From a Traveler by Pierre Teilhard de Chardin. Copyright 1962 in the English translation by William

Collins Sons & Co., Ltd., London, and Harper & Row, Publishers, Inc., New York. Copyright 1956, 1957, by Editions Bernard Grasset, Paris.

The Making of a Mind by Pierre Teilhard de Chardin. Copyright 1961 by Editions Bernard Grasset, Paris. Copyright 1965 in the English translation by William Collins Sons & Co., Ltd., London, and Harper & Row, Publishers, Inc., New York.

The Phenomenon of Man by Pierre Teilhard de Chardin. Copyright 1955 by Editions du Seuil. Copyright 1959 by William Collins Sons & Co., Ltd., London, and Harper & Row, Publishers, Inc., New York. *Note:* Reprint only from 1965 Torchbook edition.

The Vision of the Past by Pierre Teilhard de Chardin. Copyright 1966 in the English translation by William Collins Sons & Co., Ltd., London, and Harper & Row, Publishers, Inc., New York. Copyright 1957 by Editions du Seuil, Paris.

Throughout this work, references to the writings of Teilhard de Chardin appear under the following abbreviations:

AM — *The Appearance of Man*
BE — *Building the Earth*
DM — *The Divine Milieu*
FM — *The Future of Man*
HU — *Hymn of the Universe*
LT — *Letters From a Traveler*
MM — *The Making of a Mind*
PH — *The Phenomenon of Man*
VP — *The Vision of the Past*

CONTENTS

	Introduction	15
1.	In the Spirit of St. Thomas Aquinas	17
2.	A Transfigued Universe	29
3.	Christ in the Universe	39
4.	Christian Optimism and the Last Things	53
5.	The Parousia	59
6.	Teilhard and the Franciscan School	69
7.	Teilhard and Modern Thought	83
8.	The Method of Teilhard	95
9.	Overlooked Aspects of Teilhard's Thought	113
	Epilogue	127
	Glossary of Interrelated Terms	133
	Selected Index	151

ASPECTS OF THE THOUGHT
OF
TEILHARD DE CHARDIN

INTRODUCTION

Each of these essays takes up an aspect of the many-sided thought of Pierre Teilhard de Chardin. The essays are presented in such a way that the reader may read any or all of them in whatever order he chooses. A few of the writings have been published before as articles in periodicals.

The common theme that runs throughout these pages is the favorite motif of Teilhard—the presence of God in the universe through His creative power. Teilhard's keen awareness of the divine immanence in nature is linked to his deep appreciation of the grandeur of the creature in the sight of God and men. This twofold intuition of the famed Jesuit allies him with quite divergent schools of thought—with St. Thomas Aquinas, with St. Bonaventure, and with the process philosophies of modern times.

The key concept in Teilhard which brings together these views is, of course, *evolution.* Evolution is at once the creature in progress towards a divine goal; and at the same time, evolution is the creative power and intelligence of God working from within His creation to the manifestation of His glory, which is the well-being of the universe as a whole. The final purpose of the evolutionary movement is the consciousness of its divine origin and destiny in and through man, who attains this goal, in the Providence of God, in union with the God-Man, Jesus

Christ. Such a divine destiny, however, would be totally beyond the natural powers either of the universe or of mankind, if left to their own resources. Hence the necessary recognition of the divine transcendence—God's superior power at work within nature itself—to achieve the unattainable destiny. Inasmuch as that superior power produces tangible and visible results in natural and human history, it invites study and interpretation on the part of men, who, caught up in the evolutionary spiral, now must give conscious direction to the powers and forces that, under the divine impulse, have brought mankind to the present decisive moment of history.

These essays are the result of several seminars conducted at Don Bosco College, Newton, New Jersey. The author expresses his thanks to all who made possible their publication, especially to Nino Cavoto, John Itzaina, Michael McDonald, Thomas Schulte, and Carl Tershak for valuable work contributed.

1.

IN THE SPIRIT OF ST. THOMAS AQUINAS

Teilhard de Chardin once explained the purpose of his system in three points. First, he wrote, his aim was to develop a correct physics and metaphysics of evolution. The world we know is not developing by chance. Secondly, he continued, if the world is not developing by chance, it is necessary to postulate an *immanent* finality in the universe. This finality must be structurally controlled by a Personal Center. This Center is not merely the "Unmoved Mover" of Aristotle, but God who became Man in Christ. Thirdly, the last end of the universe is God's glory in and through Christ, and for the attainment of this goal, human effort is necessary. Teilhard expressed these ideas in a very short summary which he wrote in 1936 in response to a request from the Apostolic Delegate in China. He entitled his statement "Some Reflections on the Conversion of the World." He wrote in part:

> A first step would consist in developing (along the lines of the "perennial philosophy": primacy of being, act and potency) a correct physics and metaphysics of evolution. I am convinced that an honest interpretation of the new achievements of scientific thought justifiably leads not to a materialistic but to a spiritualistic interpretation of evolution:—the world we know is not developing by chance, but is structurally

controlled by a personal Center of Universal convergence.[1]

The outlook of Teilhard simultaneously combined certainties derived from science, from reason, and from faith. Mindful that the Angelic Doctor was a genius of synthesis, many contemporary followers of Thomas seem to agree today that an authentic Thomistic vision of the 20th century ought—from the very method employed by St. Thomas himself—to take into account truths known from science, from philosophy, and from faith. As a matter of fact, the very plan of the *Summa,* far from isolating natural, human, and divine knowledge, makes use of all three as in marvellous succession it considers creation, the incarnation, and the consummation of all things in Christ, Who is the model of human activity, by which man attains his end.

This is not to suggest a coincidence of *content* between the doctrine of St. Thomas as developed in the *Summa* and the thought of Teilhard. But certainly there is some resemblance in their overall method of procedure, some similarity of approach, and a like goal. No less an authority than Cardinal Danielou has stated that certain basic themes in Teilhard are closely allied with Thomistic thought.

The three steps of Teilhard, mentioned in the previous paragraphs, are examples of such themes. Involved in Teilhard's first step, as enunciated above, we have the following points: the primacy of being, the understanding of change in terms of act and potency, the importance of finality in a world of change. We will return to this

---

[1] Quoted by Henri de Lubac, *Teilhard Explained.* (New York: Paulist Press, 1968), p. 42.

point. Teilhard's second step is to find a Personal Center of the universe—this Personal Center he identifies with Christ; and he sees all the unity, truth and goodness in the world in greater depth because related to Christ. In a sense, he presents for our consideration a twofold vision—the vision of the universe in evolution and the vision of evolution as related to God in Christ. The universe at once enjoys its own autonomy, yet moves towards the Divine Destiny of its own existence. We might call this a vivid appreciation of the twofold *analogy* of being. For, the reality of each thing in the world, and indeed the whole world, has been enhanced by the Incarnation and is directed towards a finality which is divine: the "analogy of being" (the similarity and relationship of all things to God) is now transfigured; and the transfiguration is occurring in time. It becomes visible to the discerning eye.

How? The meaning of the "analogy of being" for St. Thomas is that each thing is something similar to God according to its capacity. And, at the same time, each thing is related to God as effect to Cause and therefore essentially depends upon God. In the vision of Teilhard, the preceding statements are taken, not merely in an abstract way, but in a concrete sense and in the context of an evolving universe. Teilhard speaks of the "divine diaphany." By this he means that he *sees*, i.e., feels and knows by connaturality, that each thing reveals God because it is similar to Him. God "appears" to him in and through things. This holds true, not only as far as individual things are concerned, but for the whole universe, which is a great manifestation of God's power and therefore of God Himself. Furthermore, in a similarly vivid sense, Teilhard takes the universal "dependence" of each thing and of the whole universe upon God. Thus, since for him the whole universe is in evolution, he keenly appreciates the fact that the entire evolutionary movement is now, has been, and will be literally *dependent* upon God's continuing direction. This is the meaning of the "Omega Point," which is at once the beginning and end of evolution as well as a Living Person, here and now controlling the evolutionary growth. By faith Teilhard knows that this Living Person has appeared in history as Jesus Christ.

In such a perspective, in his final step, Teilhard easily envisions the goal of evolution. This goal is God's glory, understood in terms of human progress towards the final transfiguration of the universe and the attainment of eternal life by the human race at the end of time. But all this would be impossible without a build-up of the universe and of the human species through a complex process, in which *relationship, human personality,* and *social consciousness* all play an important part. No one would underestimate these concepts in Thomistic philosophy, and their clear understanding can help immensely towards a deeper appreciation of Teilhard's thought.

Cosmogenesis: A Universe in Process

The starting point of philosophy for St. Thomas Aquinas is the recognition of reality—of a world distinct from the thinker—which presents itself to the senses and which invites rational analysis. And St. Thomas claims that the world, though *real* (or "being"), is not pure being but *changing* being, which he explains through act and potency. Reality not only *is;* but it is active: it *becomes.* The more

In the Spirit of St. Thomas Aquinas

we come to know its capacity (potency) for change, the better we will understand it.

Teilhard's great insight builds upon this intuition shared by St. Thomas. His one objective is *to see,* to see the world as it is. What Teilhard sees is a world in evolution. It is his conviction that everything in the world—plants, animals, man—has been in a steady process of evolution from the very first instant of creation. Nothing can suddenly come to light after various stages of evolution that was not in some form present—even if unknown—from the very beginning. There was an inner driving force— what Teilhard labeled the "within" of things—compelling each thing to seek its own development, perfection and destiny. This shows up not only in man, but in the drive for perfection of plants, animals and insects, all of which developed certain exterior characteristics. After the development of the massive brain and intricate nervous system in the primates, this species ceased striving for exterior development and allowed the "within" itself to develop. Out of this species, suddenly came man. With his appearance, the evolutionary urge in the non-human branches waned, because the peak of biological evolution had been attained. This past history gives Teilhard a clue for the future. He sees all of creation as working its way up from a broad base at the beginning (which he terms "Point Alpha") and spiralling up toward its ultimate destiny (which he calls "Point Omega"). This evolutionary process still continues in man, but on a mental level rather than a physical one, and in conjunction with other men rather than alone. Mass communications, swift transportation, international governing bodies such as the United Nations are signs of this development. The object of all man's mental energies is Point Omega, which already exists and which from the beginning of time has been attracting thinking man to himself. Point Omega is identical with Point Alpha, i.e., God, from Whom creation originally came. Through evolution, this creation has culminated in man; and it aims at the return of thinking beings to God, through the God-Made-Man in the person of Jesus of Nazareth. Natural evolution must eventually converge with the new and developing (supernatural) order inserted into history through Christianity, whose central axis is the Catholic Church.

We are far from suggesting that the foregoing principles correspond to the Cosmology of St. Thomas Aquinas. But we are proposing that this vision of Teilhard is not opposed to the metaphysical principles of Aquinas. Basically, Teilhard perceives a "within" and a "without" of things, which sometimes are called by the names, "radial" and "tangential" energy. Energy is the most primitive form of universal stuff. In much the same way that Aquinas sees all things in terms of varying "act," Teilhard conceives everything in terms of "energy." It has been suggested by some interpreters that one instance of "within" of things is the suprasensible, dynamic principle which St. Thomas calls the substantial form. The "without" of things, on the other hand, corresponds to the external and accidental manifestations (forms) of the activity and inter-activity among things. But Teilhard never considers such manifestations in isolation from actual reality which is a closely knit whole, brought together into varying degrees of unity through a vast network of real, accidental relationships.

A more difficult problem arises, however, when we

consider Teilhard's contention that all reality is basically one, from which develop the various structures (material and spiritual) which we observe in the world. Indeed, radial energy in its various manifestations seems to presuppose (in Teilhard's conception) a fundamental thrust implanted in the universe in virtue of which reality develops and diversifies, while retaining a basic unity of origin and end. It is almost as if there is a "soul of the world" animating the whole; and all developments (material and spiritual alike) seem to be accidental manifestations of the one reality. So stated, we have outright pantheism. Is there any other interpretation possible?

We suggest that the "thrust" in the universe is the created dynamic force which manifests God's immanence and creative power in nature. Since radial energy is that form of energy which accounts for cosmic evolution towards the more complex, the more aware, the more spiritual, it would seem that in its basic form it is the creative power of God Himself. Thomistic philosophy has always taught that God is present to His creation and co-operates in each creature's activity. Furthermore, such presence of God is wholly in the whole creation and wholly in each part. The tangible effect of God's presence in the case of each creature is the creature itself. What, if any, is the tangible effect of God's presence in the universe as a whole? Teilhard seems to suggest a creative force, by which God unites the whole world and gives it a forward drive to perfection. It is like the "elan vital" of Bergson. Does this imprison God in the universe? No, certainly. No more than God's presence in the soul through sanctifying grace imprisons Him. His presence through grace is a new manner of presence with a created effect. So,

God's presence in the whole universe as its directing Providence has its corresponding effect, which is the creative force of the universe. This creative force is God's own presence as manifested in His *whole* creation as its guiding principle. From it, both the sensible manifestations of matter and the superior appearance of spirit proceed. Thus, the "Unmoved Mover" of Aristotle exerts a visible and diversified *influence* in the world. This influence is not God, as if identified with nature, or as its soul, but the over-all and under-all *creative* effect of His immanence and presence to the world.

Teilhard insists that this immanence and presence is something tangible and phenomenal, i.e., presenting some physical, sensible trace discoverable and even evident to the discerning scientist. From a Thomistic point of view, the question we must ask is this: "What is the effect of God's providence, God's immanence, and God's presence to the world, as applied to the universe as a whole?" Teilhard's answer would seem to be that it is the *growth* of the universe as such. But the growth of the universe is the real and discernible progress of evolution itself, just as the effect of God's presence to individual things is the creature itself; and just as the effect of their proper activity is the manifestation of His concurrence. Thus, God's presence in the universe as a whole is something measureable, something that has been manifested, and something that continues to endure. It is the tangible manifestation of God's over-all presence, immanence and concurrence in creaturely activity. It reveals *God Himself* working in and through His creatures. To use Teilhard's own phrase, it is God making things make themselves.

This vision of God's immanence in the world—an immanence misinterpreted by philosophers such as Alexander, Whitehead, and others—must not overlook God's transcendence. God *in Himself* remains the completely Other (Infinite), but in as much as He has created the world and is present in it, He makes Himself known *to us* in this fashion. Without rejecting in any sense God's revelation to man through faith, without neglecting man's understanding of God through reason, Teilhard seeks to know God by knowing the world insofar as it is a manifestation of God. He wishes to determine how God acts in developing the world, and to study the direction towards which God's action points. Thus, the study of the world and its evolution is simultaneously a study of God's finite manifestation of Himself and of His providence in directing it towards its end.

What is more Thomistic than the concept of God as the "Prime Mover" influencing the activity of the world? Who more than St. Thomas insists on God's providence and concurrence in His creature's action, yet maintaining the autonomy of creaturely activity? Teilhard transfers these concepts to a global field of reference. God influences not only the individual's activity. He concurs also in the over-all direction of the universe as a whole, to which He is present as much as to the individual parts. And this direction is nothing else than evolution—the over-all manifestation of a divine finality in the world. Thus, Providence is not an abstraction. It is the visible direction that the universe is taking under the divine impulse. Or, more concretely, it *is* God directing the whole of His creation through His creative force. It is not that God is reduced to the world. But the world or creation cannot be fully and clearly understood until it is seen as the very action (*ad extra*) of God

Christian Optimism

Teilhard's vision of the world as the continuing work of God gives rise to an all-pervading optimism, which certainly is not foreign to the world-view of St. Thomas, as we will presently point out.

Oftentimes the objection is made that Teilhard fails to give proper place in his thought to the existence of evil in the world. To some extent, this is certainly true, as even the most favorable commentators of Teilhard readily admit. But we ought not to be distracted by this lacuna from the positive message that Teilhard is teaching our contemporary world. Teilhard's vision is directed over the span of many centuries. He is totally convinced that the work of God cannot fail. The directing presence of God-Omega, Who is identified with Jesus Christ, the God-Man, cannot be frustrated. The finality of evolution, as realized up to this time, has not been spared the counter-influences of various types of evil. But evil cannot overwhelm God. Nor can man, cooperating with the plan of God as revealed in Jesus Christ, ultimately succumb to evil. The future lies in the power of those who believe in the goodness of God and of man. No obstacle—not all the powers of hell put together, not the combined antichristian forces of atheism and human malice accumulated over the centuries—can prevail over the determined Will of God to save mankind. It is this Christian sense of direction and of hope that Teilhard wishes the Christian community to share with all mankind.

In the Spirit of St. Thomas Aquinas

Far from being foreign to the thought of St. Thomas Aquinas, this vision might well be considered a 20th century version of the "philosophia perennis," transferred from a stationary stance to a world recognized to be in evolution. In the Thomistic philosophy we are given, so to speak, a "still" picture of reality as related to God. In many ways, it is an analysis of the many and various things of the world understood as separate and distinct entities, each with its own autonomy, meaning and purpose. Each thing in the world shares in the fact that it *IS*, that it is subject to change, that it is related to other things in manifold ways, and that it has more or less perfection according to its position up the ladder of being, at whose summit stands the Supreme Being, Who is All-Perfect. Teilhard shifts his gaze from individual things to the *Whole Universe*. As it were, he gives us a *Moving Picture* of the great panorama of reality depicted in single strokes by St. Thomas. The universe, as a whole, is seen to be autonomous, meaningful, and purposeful. The whole universe is *Moving Forward* through evolution from a less perfect to a more perfect condition, notwithstanding the presence of evil in the world and even its relative increase. Through man, there is an increase in complexity-consciousness in the world, because of the developing relationships among men themselves and their constant discovery of new relationships existing between the various things of the world. Meanwhile, modern man has become conscious of an upward thrust that impels him forward to an Unknown Point which seems to draw mankind on to ultimate perfection, in spite of the personal and social ills in the world. Teilhard argues that this Point is a Divine Person Who has revealed Himself in history and Who calls all mankind to progress to its ultimate destiny of deification. The Source of the radial energy which accounts for evolution is not distinct from the Love that has revealed Himself in time in the Person of Christ and in the Person of the Holy Spirit, Who by a higher form of "radial energy," viz., *grace,* leads mankind forward also on a supernatural level.

2.

A TRANSFIGURED UNIVERSE

Some aspects of Teilhard's thought present serious problems for Christian thinkers.* For one thing, the distinction between matter and spirit tends to be blurred in his thought. For another, how is the natural related to the supernatural? Clearly, Teilhard's whole purpose is to fuse into a basic unity the various distinctions traditional in the perennial philosophy: matter and spirit, nature and supernature, love of the world and love of God. The serious problem is to "fuse" without confusing.

On the one hand we must hold to the diversity in nature between matter and spirit. Therefore, we cannot attribute spiritual power to matter, if we take these conceptions in a strict and literal sense. On the other hand we must recognize the actual powers of nature as we find it in the world, attributing its dynamic to intrinsic causes.

In a wider perspective the question arises: to what extent can the spiritual and supernatural become evident in their effects on matter? Can there be a kind of phenomenology of the spiritual? This essay is an attempt to answer these questions.

---

*This essay is reprinted from *Chicago Studies,* Spring, 1968, pp. 101-108. Slight changes from the original have been made.

The Spiritual Power of Matter

In his evolutionary theory Teilhard speaks of "the spiritual power of matter." The phrase is reminiscent of the philosophy of Henri Bergson, who envisions an "elan vital" or vital impulse at the basis of evolutionary development. This principle is somewhat identified with God, although it is not clear to what extent. Is the conception of an "elan vital" or of a "spiritual power in matter" compatible with "perennial philosophy?"

The following considerations suggest an affirmative answer to the question. This answer is developed according to the principle followed usually in theological matters—the analogy of faith. But here, instead of proceeding from a matter of faith to another matter of faith, we intend to proceed from a matter of faith to a philosophical hypothesis.

The theologians speak of supernatural, sanctifying grace as a divine gift, by which God is present to the soul in a supernatural way. It is a gift, resulting in effects which are not due to a created nature,—God's presence in a new way. God becomes present to the spiritual creature in a way that is above the natural power or potency of such a creature. It is a completely supernatural situation. It is the communication of divine life to a spiritual being which of itself is incapable of generating such life.

Theologians conceive of sanctifying grace as being infused into the soul by God at Baptism. As a result of this infusion, the soul possesses a new principle of life and activity over and above its natural status, over and above everything that is naturally due to its nature. In virtue of this new life, the person stands in a new relationship to God, no longer a simple creature of God but an adopted son. Consequently, the person is loved by God in a special way and is enabled to love God as Father. Because of its new orientation towards God, the soul receives the power to act towards a goal beyond its natural capacities in the attaining of God's own life in heaven. Hence grace is called the seed of eternal life. It is a divinization of the creature. Saint Peter calls it a "participation in the divine nature." By this "participation" God becomes immanent to his creature. Nevertheless, the natural immanence of God through his ordinary conservation and concurrence remains intact. God becomes immanent in a new way; and all the natural activities of the person continue as before. But henceforth they have a new direction because of the changed condition of their agent. We may say that the person is in a radically transformed condition, although the effects of this transformation are not immediately visible and they will achieve fulfillment only in the next life.

Could there be a similar situation on another level of reality? I do not mean a communication of grace as such to matter. This would be impossible, since God's supernatural gift of Himself through grace can be communicated only to an intelligent creature. But I am suggesting an "analogue" of grace. Could there be in matter a principle superior to its nature? As a result of this, matter would be in a radically transformed condition, although this would not be immediately apparent. In fact, the full achievement of this transformation could take place only at the end of time.

An Analogue of Grace

I am suggesting that in the very heart of nature from the

beginning of time, there has been the *creative power* of God *in the concrete* (not merely in an abstract sense)—power in itself superior to matter and, properly speaking, of the order of spirit. Like sanctifying grace, this "analogue" of grace would make God present in a unique, though not supernatural way. His presence would be in a way unsuspected for irrational creatures. This real, creative power would then account for "divine" activity in matter, i.e., for activity seemingly over and above the natural powers and exigencies of inert matter. In this conception, there would be almost nothing inconceivable as happening in matter. So viewed, the created universe stands in a new relationship to God, ordained intrinsically to the divine will in a way not due to its nature. As such it is an object of divine complacency in as much as it tends through its own activity towards "a new heaven and a new earth" which God has set for its destiny.

Just as it is (naturally) inconceivable that a created spirit might be divinized, so it might be granted that we should not naturally expect matter to be in any sense "divinized" in this lesser way. We know of the divinization of rational creatures through revelation. We might conjecture or conclude to the "divinization" or "spiritualization" of matter by the observation of power within nature beyond the range of its own expected and recognized competency. Is this what pantheistic philosophers have sensed in matter, confusing God's presence (both ordinary and "extraordinary" in the sense now suggested) with God Himself? Is this what the evolutionists have been baffled by, even the Marxists who have been so enthralled with matter? They have passed beyond matter and recognized its superior power; they should have proceeded one step further—from the mysterious "analogue" of God to God Himself, the omnipotent giver.

If we adopt this point of view, the whole process of natural development and its relationship to the supernatural take on a new aspect. At the end of all history and development stands the Risen Lord of the Transfiguration drawing all things to Himself. But He does so, not merely by drawing matter from without. No, from within the hidden recesses of matter itself, there surges the impulse of a divinely implanted urge in virtue of which the whole creation is in travail until it effects its own triumphant transfiguration by which God will be "all in all."

I conceive the original creation of God as constituted in being through its own material and formal principles (substantial and accidental), leaving open to the discovery of philosophy and science a more detailed description of this original creature of God in the material order. But I conceive it as immediately raised by the divine power to a condition superior to its condition as matter. By the creative power of God, the "analogue" of grace (i.e., the "vital impulse" of Bergson or the "Spiritual Power" of Teilhard, call it what you will), I conceive this creature of God as ordained from the start to the divine order (as far as this is possible for a material being as such) through this marvellous free gift of God by which God Himself is present to matter in an unsuspected way, directing it towards even higher heights without intervention at each new stage of development. Through this creative power, God is present to matter in a mysterious, unfathomable way, similar to (but inferior to) His gratuitous presence in the soul by sanctifying grace.

And as in the supernatural order "the spirit breathes

where He wills," so in the natural order (in virtue of this creative and superior principle) God heads the whole creation "where He wills" to the inscrutable manifestations of His glory.

Phenomenology of the Spirit

The basic manifestation of God's glory is the presence in the world of God's intelligent creature, man, capable of coming to know and love God through the knowledge and love of His material creation. Notwithstanding the fundamental power of man to reach this goal, God saw fit to help him to reach not only this but even a higher goal, revealing Himself to man in a special and supernatural way, especially through the appearance in the world of His Son, Our Lord Jesus Christ, and through the mission in Christ's Mystical Body, the Church, of His own Holy Spirit.

Similarly, while the material universe has the capacity to reach its own objectives by its own inherent powers, God is directing it to a transfiguration and glorification not due it.

In the course of time the mysterious plan of God unfolds itself. This plan is summed up on the phrase of St. Paul: to re-establish all things in Christ—those in the heavens and those on the earth. Although the objective is to be fully achieved only after the second coming of Christ at the end of time, meanwhile there is a build-up of His Mystical Body on earth. Thus, we must recognize the tremendous truth that humanity (and through humanity, all creation), is plunged in space-time duration in order to provide Christ with the material for His Body, in an analogous way that Mary provided the flesh and blood for the physical Christ.

The visible effects of this over-all plan of God are observable in human history, in the establishment, growth and sufferings of Christians over the face of the earth. The consciousness of the inevitable victory of God's plan, amid ever so many difficulties, must be reckoned as an important contributing factor to the realization of the goal itself. Simultaneously, the manifestation of the fulfilling of God's plan necessarily occurs. Furthermore, the expectation of further fulfillment and manifestation is not only in order, but a requisite for the development itself. Without pretending to predict the complicated details of the future, the Christian nevertheless should expect to come to an ever clearer realization of the meaning of the plan that God has set in motion, not merely from the appearance of Christ on earth, but from the very beginning of time.

It is not natural to suppose that this development should occur on the material as well as spiritual levels, on the natural as well as supernatural plane? Such a supposition is a basic conviction of Teilhard. If this point of view is accepted, then a convergence of the various lines of development within the natural and supernatural spheres seems inevitable. Hence we should expect that God's evolving plan will become more and more evident to observers, even on a phenomenological level. Not only human history itself but all of nature (if raised up to a supernatural destiny) should be driven to its goal from within—a direction that necessarily becomes manifest as the centuries pass on.

The thought of Teilhard de Chardin, and the reappraisals of traditional thought that it provokes, can be an important asset here. Or at least so it seems to the present writer. The optimism with which Teilhard views the universe could be the spark to enkindle a new vision of the universe, born of the desire to understand and fulfill God's plan in creation, with a genuine love for the universe and for man, which we should conceive as endowed not only with their natural goods, but with the very presence of the Spirit of God, Who through His grace and through His vital impulse leads the universe to its destiny of re-establishment in Christ.

Antidote For Our Times

If we compare our times with those of St. Thomas Aquinas, we can recognize similarities among the many differences. Aquinas was anxious to incorporate the insights of Aristotle into his Christian vision of the world. However, he did this against the background of a well-established Augustinianism whose proponents in some respects were bitterly anti-Aristotelian, even though they themselves were to some extent influenced by the rediscovery of Aristotelian thought. Aristotle's thought overemphasized the transcendence of God and neglected His immanence in the creation—an essential part of the philosophical outlook of St. Augustine.

Today we find that the presence or immanence of God in the world is almost completely overlooked against the background of the marvelous discoveries of the modern age. God is far away—"God is dead" as far as the thought of many contemporaries go. Do we not need to restore the sense of the presence of God in the face of the prevalent agnosticism and secularism of our day? One way to do this is to restore the consciousness of God's hand at work within the very recesses of nature itself. Teilhard's point of view certainly concentrates on this objective. On the other hand, some modern philosophers (such as Bergson and Whitehead) adopt a similar viewpoint. Should the insights of these philosophers be lost, especially since the sense of God's immanence has been lost in the world at large? We need to remind the world of God's immanence to it not only in the ordinary sense of conservation and concurrence with individual things, but also in the over-all way that impressed men like Bergson and Teilhard. We are not, of course, suggesting a neglect of God's transcendence. But a genuine appreciation of His immanence will lead to a deeper realization of His transcendence.

Teilhard looked upon the world with eyes full of wonder over the intrinsic power of nature to progress and develop. Yet behind all this development he saw a "spiritual power," a vital impulse within matter indicative of God's special presence. In virtue of this presence, all development will ultimately culminate at the end of time in the transfiguration of the world in Christ. Can we not similarly combine these two points of view of immanence and transcendence? We easily apply the two concepts to God. It is imperative to apply the two concepts to God's creation.

God is superior to His creation and He is leading it to a supernatural goal. God is immanent to His creation and provides that creation itself moves to the pre-destined Goal beyond itself. In both cases He makes use of created reality—the created humanity of our Lord Jesus Christ which has already reached its glorification and is transcendent to the world. But through His continuing presence in the world—He is immanent, through the Eucharist and through His Holy Spirit in the church. Teilhard suggests another mysterious immanence which, while within nature, stretches beyond its natural confines. It is this mysterious immanence, this "analogue of grace," this "spiritual power," this divine "vital impulse" within nature that we have tried to single out in this essay.

Christian faith teaches us to love our neighbor because he has the seed of future glory impressed within his soul through sanctifying grace. We of the Christian faith should not forget, however, that even in the natural order man is made in the image and likeness of God, which accounts for his intrinsic value. The modern world is well aware of this value. Similarly, the world has become cognizant of the intrinsic powers of nature and has come to value them highly. Cannot Christians learn this lesson from their contemporaries? Teilhard's thought challenges us in this respect; but his challenge is not merely to love the world for the sake of the world but to love it for its mysterious relationship to God-Omega, because it has within it the seed of its future glory.*

---

*The question may be asked: What is the difference between God's presence to the universe as a whole, as brought out in the first essay, and the "extraordinary" divine presence described in the second essay? Actually it is the same divine presence under two different aspects. In the first essay, we emphasize that God's presence in the world is an over-all presence as well as a presence to individual things. This is a re-statement, with an added emphasis, to a commonly held teaching of the Schools. The second essay deals more with our *knowledge* and *realization* of God's immanence in the world. There is a cosmic energy in the world, due to the divine presence, which achieves results even on the *phenomenal* level, compelling us to recognize a superior power in nature which transcends material forces.

3.

CHRIST IN THE UNIVERSE

A central idea in the thought of Teilhard de Chardin is the pre-eminence of Christ in the universe.* This conception, in itself, has a firm basis in St. Paul. Teilhard, however, takes the Pauline passages in support of this idea in a literal sense. Furthermore, he understands them in such a way as to make Christ the very center of his own (i.e., Teilhard's) evolving universe. Fr. Christopher Mooney develops this aspect of Teilhard's thought in chapter three of his book, *Teilhard de Chardin and the Mystery of Christ.* Our purpose here is to review Teilhard's point of view against the background of certain points of traditional teaching, so as to appreciate better the authenticity of the insight.

We are not dealing here with the question of the primacy of Christ in the supernatural order. Neither is there question of Christ's constant salvific action through the centuries on behalf of the whole world through His Church. There *is* question as to how Christ's action fits into the natural evolution of man and the universe. This is precisely the question that enticed Teilhard de Chardin. Our

---

*This essay is reprinted, with slight modifications, from *Emmanuel,* April, 1967, pp. 160-167.

purpose, then, is in the spirit of Teilhard to see if we can find some clue of the presence of Christ in the "phenomena" of the evolution and progress of man. Natural science —to a great extent ignorant of Christ—is aware of such evolution and progress. Modern philosophy is also aware of "process" and "development," for which it seeks in its own way for a rational explanation. It is only proper that those who have the gift of Faith should study the same "phenomena" and in the light of both faith and reason give some explanation. Then, starting from premises which the scientist and philosopher admit, they may go on to a wider horizon and view. Hence, our present article is directed, not to scientists and philosophers, but to those accustomed in their understanding of reality to join faith with reason.

Three "Explosions"

Einstein detected three enormous undertones within today's historical ramifications: the biological, the atomic (scientific-technological) and the psychological—the explosions that now shake our world in staggering transformation. The first of these "explosions" has to do with the growth of life on the planet, the second with man's control over nature, and the third with man's knowledge of his own psyche. Taken together, the latter two are sometimes referred to as the "knowledge explosion."

Regarding biological evolution, no one was more convinced than Teilhard de Chardin, whose many years of labor contributed to a clearer understanding of this subject. He was convinced that there is "spiritual power" in matter to account for the rise and growth of life over the

A. Magid

Dear Colleague:

Thanks to a grant from the Fund
of distinguished scholars will
November. They will address th

Sex, Gender, and Humanity:

An advance announcement of thi
Please note that the series in
history, film, art history, poe
You may wish to incorporate on

1. I experience the world in a certain way
2. how do I explain the experience
   a. chance, infinite regress
   → b. infinite cause, intelligence
3. b satisfies reason
4. posit the cause
   "God"

earth. We might compare this force in the universe accounting for evolution to the elan vital or vital impulse of Bergson. At the beginning of time, to put it simply, we must recognize the *creative power* of God as a *real* factor in the developing of the universe. We can compare this creative power to the gratuitous gift of grace in the supernatural order. Just as grace makes God present in a new way to the spiritual creature, so this creative principle in matter makes God present in an unsuspected way, working immanently from within nature for the origin and development of life on succeeding levels.

By this creative power or life-principle, the whole universe is conditioned to fulfill God's own purpose in creation. Divine Revelation tells us that this purpose is the immortality of the human race united with Christ as in one Mystical Body—a purpose to be achieved only at the end of time, when God's original gift of immortality to man will be regained in the General Resurrection. Meanwhile, according to Teilhard, mankind evolves toward an ever greater consciousness until finally, notwithstanding the death penalty that has been inflicted on men after original sin, mankind will be restored forever in Christ at His Second Coming. Thus, the ultimate fruit of the elan vital, or life-principle, in conjunction with Christ as Head of the Mystical Body, is unending life with God in heaven.

We will return to this point before the end of this essay. Meanwhile, we must consider that there has been more than one kind of evolution in the universe. There has been the "knowledge explosion" resulting in man's ever-increasing knowledge and control of nature and his increased knowledge of his own psyche. Does Christ's presence enter into this development too? If we follow along the lines of thought of Teilhard de Chardin, such progress might well be attributed to a "Christic presence" in the universe. Teilhard found proof of this Christic presence in very definite texts of St. Paul.

The Cosmic Presence of Christ

Regarding Christ, St. Paul writes that "in Him all things hold together" (Colossians 1:17). He ascended "above all the heavens, that He might fill all things" (Ephesians 4:9). For Paul, indeed, Christ is "all things and in all" (Colossians 3:11).

Teilhard insisted that the "cosmic presence" of Christ must be seen in conjunction with His Resurrection. According to him, the Resurrection is that "tremendous cosmic event" which inaugurates the actual exercise by Christ of His function as physical center by which, in the words of St. Paul, he "fills all things."

In the words of Teilhard: "The presence of the Word Incarnate penetrates everything as a universal element. At the heart of all things it shines as a centre infinitely intimate and yet at the same time (because it coincides with the consummation of the universe) infinitely far away.... Everything around us is physically *Christified* and can become so more and more." The universal presence of Christ is somehow irrevocably linked to God's own omnipresence. Omnipresence, in fact, means the presence of Christ, who through His humanity is the active center radiating all those energies which lead the universe back to God. "The Divine immensity has transformed itself for us into the omnipresence of Christification."

We are dealing here, not with the supernatural presence of Christ to the world as the Head of the Mystical Body, but with an even more universal and cosmic presence. Yet this presence is not the ordinary presence of God in individual things "through His essence, through His knowledge, and through His power," of which Philosophy speaks. Indeed, Christ in His humanity could not partake of such a fundamental presence in the world, which pre-existed the humanity of Christ. If, then, this presence of Christ in the world is not a supernatural one, nor a natural one, how are we to conceive it?

Here we must return to a conception developed in several of these essays. In order to vindicate Teilhard's conception of the material universe evolving towards an end above its natural destiny, we can picture in the heart of matter an "analogue of grace," an "elan vital," or a divine impulse indicative of God's actual presence in an extraordinary and new way, gratuitously immanent to matter and directing it towards God's designs. It is nothing else than God's creative power *in action.* We now suggest that this creative power in matter, after the Resurrection of Christ, appropriately became His own instrument in the directing of the universe towards His Second Coming. So, we are suggesting two things: (1) the Triune God (Father, Son and Holy Spirit) is present in matter through the "analogue of grace" of which we have spoken; (2) in this presence we ought to envision the Second Person as joined with His Risen Humanity, literally controlling the universe in a unique and preternatural way.

It is this presence of God and of Christ in nature by which we can account for the extraordinary evolution of the world and of man—an evolution which has caused wonder to scientists and philosophers alike. Only such a presence, a genuine "divine impulse" enables us adequately to explain evolution in its various manifestations. With it, we can reasonably account for the progress of evolution not only on a purely biological basis, but in man's scientific and psychological development.

To understand this, we must consider the nature of human knowledge. Logic tells us of three operations by which men ordinarily attain knowledge: abstraction, judgment, and reasoning. But there is another source of knowledge, which is called "knowledge by connaturality" which is somewhat extraordinary and to a great extent unexplored. It is to explain this kind of knowledge and its development that we have recourse to the presence of God and Christ in nature.

The most outstanding example of knowledge by connaturality is mystical knowledge, when someone knows God through love better than any philosopher or theologian, yet in a way beyond concepts or words; "known as though unknown," in the words of St. Thomas.

In the supposition of the "analogue of grace" or divine impulse indicative of God's extraordinary presence in the universe, this mystical experience would be quite possible to man even before the coming of Christ. However, after the Resurrection of Christ, mystical experience becomes more obvious and prevalent on the supernatural level in the Church, because of grace, making Christ present as the very Life of the Soul.

Knowledge by connaturality is not limited to mystical knowledge. It includes esthetic knowledge involved in the cultural development of man through the centuries. In a word, it encompasses any knowledge based on the lived experience of the truth, the living contact of the intellect with reality itself, overlaid with elements from the affective or feeling side of man's nature. The knowledge we gain through love of any kind well exemplifies this knowledge by connaturality, i.e., by sympathy or by "fellow-feeling." It is extraordinary inasmuch as it involves more than an ordinary intellectual act of knowledge, and it is not, therefore, expressible in concepts or judgments. Thus we speak of the "stroke of genius" of an artist, a poet, or a musician; and we say that he is "inspired" because he communicates through his work of art a vision of reality which is beyond expression in words. This is an example of "knowledge by connaturality" which is first experienced personally and then communicated to others. Finally, mental telepathy, clairvoyance, and the various forms of ESP are the most extraordinary examples of this kind of knowledge. In these cases somehow there arise out of the subconscious of the human psyche immediate intuitions or insights by which the subject knowing immediately is aware of objects "related" to the subject, but not present by ordinary evidence (sensory or intellectual). Modern Psychology is interested in exploring the future possibilities of these avenues of truth. But must we not, first of all, recognize a superior source in this kind of knowledge? Here again we might well point to the divine impulse in things which reveals an extraordinary presence of God. And if this divine impulse is considered after the Resurrection as being under the direction of the Risen Christ, past progress in this extraordinary type of knowledge and its future development depends on the direction of Christ immanent in nature.

Up to now, philosophers have overlooked any such preternatural presence of Christ in nature. But the thought of Teilhard de Chardin, with emphasis on the "cosmic presence" of Christ points to it as a fact which suggests perhaps that Adam's preternatural gift of infused knowledge is gradually being restored by Christ's activity in the development of man's knowledge along these lines. This development is becoming more and more evident in the technological and scientific fields, which enables man to have an increasingly greater control over nature. Is there some indication here of a gradual restoration of man's original control over nature which he had as a gift from the Creator? There must be a sufficient reason for the gradual unfolding of the extraordinary powers hidden in nature, which scientific inventions, miracle drugs, and space exploration exploit to the fullest. Should Christ, immanent to nature in the sense explained, be recognized as the hidden agent to explain this development? Note well that we are not denying here that the knowledge in question is man's own and, as such, man-caused. We are referring to the *extraordinary* development of this type of knowledge in modern times, suggesting that this *providential* progress is due to an immanent and preternatural presence of Christ. Thus, the natural and mutual relationships of things among themselves and their relationship to man is the basis of this knowledge and its basic cause; but the directive influence of Christ is the cause of its wondrous development. In this case, although this development is extraordinary, it is not supernatural. Yet it is understood that if Christ is directing it, He is leading it ultimately to the supernatural. Or, to use the phrase of Teilhard, "cosmogenesis becomes Christogenesis."

Looking at things in this perspective, we find the whole

universe "Christified." This Christification must be understood as occurring on two levels of reality. First of all, it occurs on the spiritual and supernatural level. By the gift of sanctifying grace the Christian is marked with the stamp of Christ and receives his life as a member of His Mystical Body. The Mystical Body of Christ reveals Christ to the world in human history; and the invisible presence of Christ becomes more and more evident to the world with the advance of the Church throughout space and time. But Christ-life is not limited to the supernatural order. We have suggested that the whole universe is somehow marked with Christ through the "analogue of grace" or divine principle infused into matter at the beginning of time. Furthermore, this principle, after Christ's Resurrection, became the instrument and sign not only of God's presence in matter but of Christ Himself directing the universe towards its end. We may, therefore, call the "analogue of grace" or vital impulse *"Christ-Life"* immanent in matter, resembling the Christ-life of grace in the human soul. Human history, human progress, human evolution are all a manifestation of this "Christ-life" in action, moving mankind and the universe despite the opposition of the forces of evil towards the divinely-appointed restoration of all things in the God-Man.

The progress of mankind in knowledge and in his control over nature is thus seen to be due not only to the work of many men but also due to the underlying influence of the Christic presence in nature, restoring to mankind the lost gifts of intuition and nature-control. What about the other gifts of integrity and immortality? Here again the thought of Teilhard de Chardin offers us enlightening considerations.

Eucharistic Presence

Teilhard stressed very much the influence of the Eucharistic presence of Christ in the universe. It is enough to think of his "Divine Milieu" and his "Mass Over the World" to realize this.

The Eucharistic presence is, in accordance with Catholic teaching, a sacramental presence—a presence indicated by the appearances of consecrated Bread and Wine. It is a new presence of the God-Man in the world. Therefore, it is distinct from God's ordinary presence in the universe, from God's special presence through grace in the soul, and from the cosmic (preternatural) presence of Christ just described. This Eucharistic presence has an *expiatory* function as connected with Christ's sacrifice on Calvary to redeem man's soul and body from sin and from the influences of sin. At the same time it is a pledge of immortality.

Saint Ignatius, Father of the Church, described the Eucharist as the "medicine of immortality." In some mysterious way he saw It as predisposing the bodies of the Christians for a risen life in the new creation, after the Parousia, but it is also a source of incorruption here and now, because it is the sacrament of unity and charity. It is the sacrament by which the Church herself, one and holy, grows constantly in sanctity and incorruption. It is the sacrament which deepens and matures the union of Christians with one another in Christ, which sanctifies them yet further, all together, in the One Christ. And by so doing, this sacrament steeps them in His immortality, His purity, His incorruption.

This is all on the supernatural level. What about on

the natural level? Consistent with his thought, Teilhard would have us conceive a purification of the whole universe gradually occurring because of the continuing and ever-multiplying Eucharistic presence of Christ in the universe. "From the moment," he writes, "that you say 'This is my body,' not only the bread of the altar, but in a certain sense everything in the universe became yours that nourishes in our souls the life of grace and the spirit. May the chosen part of the world extend your influence over me and become more you through my effort." Similarly, he conceives that the ultimate end of the purification of the world, achieved amid all the difficulties and obstacles of the forces of evil, will effect such a transformation of mankind as to call for the Parousia, or the second coming of Christ. And conversely, earthly progress will reach its point of liberation in the "lightning of the Parousia" only if it has been Christified from the inside.

Universal Christification

We can now understand why Teilhard could write that everything around us is physically "Christified" and can become so more and more. For we can consider the process of Christification taking place on various levels of reality. *Cosmic* Christification is already achieved by the presence in the world of the "divine impulse" now under the direction of the Risen Christ. A *Eucharistic* Christification is taking place through the purification of men's bodies in Holy Communion, and the ever-increasing liberation of matter from subjection to the devil. *Human* Christification constantly increases with the growth of Christ's Mystical Body. Finally, *total* Christification must eventually be achieved by the sanctification of the whole human race and correspondingly of the whole world. Christ directs the human race and the universe in these levels of reality towards their ultimate destiny; and this directing influence of Christ's presence brings about three results: a purification of the material world; a cultural and scientific growth on the level of the human psyche; and supernatural growth of the Church. This explains, on the one hand, man's supernatural development through the Church; and on the other, his preternatural or extraordinary development through psychological and technological progress—the "knowledge explosion." But there is still another aspect of man's development, mentioned in the beginning, with which we conclude this essay.

Returning, then, to the beginning of this essay, we postulated there a life principle in nature to explain biological evolution, leading to ultimate immortality. Now, we can see that, in the total picture there are at work several distinct influences to accomplish this purpose: (1) the direction always toward higher life under the divine principle right from the beginning of time; (2) the direction of the Risen Christ united to this divine principle after His Resurrection, ordaining human life to supernatural and immortal life in Himself; (3) the mysterious influence of the Eucharistic Presence of Christ, by which He predisposes mankind and the universe to a risen and transfigured life.

Thus is provision made by Divine Providence for the restoration at the end of time of man's original immortality which was lost in Adam. But the Eucharistic Presence of God performs another function, which relates to the precious gift of integrity by which man could exercise perfect self-control over his passions, leading an immaculate life. Is it possible that such a condition, or an equivalent condition, will ever be restored to man on earth? There is no doubt that the complete restoration of this gift is reserved for eternity. Is it conceivable that, sometime before and in preparation for the Parousia, a life of genuine purity might be spread over the earth by the influence of Christ's manifold presence in the world? Can there ever be in the hearts of men a "triumph of Mary's Immaculate Heart?" In the sight of the 20th century world such a triumph seems unrealistic and impossible. Yet, if we consider things in the optimistic spirit of Teilhard, such an eventual situation is not only possible, but necessary.

In view of the universal Christic presence in the universe, in view of Christ's activity as Head of the Church, in view of the ever more influential Eucharistic Presence with its purifying effects, the world seems necessarily spurred towards this goal. Yet, as Teilhard teaches, evolution is now to some extent in the hands of men. Although the world naturally, preternaturally and supernaturally moves towards its goal, it is very necessary on man's part not only to perfect himself, but to perfect society, not only to purify himself but to purify the whole world. In union with the expiation offered constantly by the Eucharistic Christ, each man can spur the universe to its destiny—to the one, far-off divine event towards which the whole creation moves, accelerating the rate of speed by which the universe is drawn by the magnetic power of God-Omega. In this way each individual can contribute here and now to the restoration of the world in Christ, which is the pre-requisite of His Second

Coming. Thus will be made possible a "synthesized act of adoration," in which an ardent desire to conquer the world, and an ardent desire to unite ourselves to God, will unite and catch fire from each other: the vital act, specifically new, corresponding to a new terrestrial age.

4.

CHRISTIAN OPTIMISM AND THE LAST THINGS

In the preceding essay we have endeavored to see various aspects of the thought of Teilhard de Chardin in the light of traditional Catholic philosophy and to propose a reconciliation of old teaching with the progressionism of Teilhard's thoughts. This is in accordance with the sound principle: *vetera novis augere.*

Now we propose to consider Teilhard's teaching on the Last Things in the light of Catholic teaching and of the Christian experience in history.* We would like, if possible, to try to resolve a few tensions existing between his thought and traditional teaching. These tensions have been generally recognized in one way or another by the various interpreters of Teilhard's world view.

First of all, as is generally recognized, we should make clear that Teilhard shows no trace of the Chiliastic error which taught that there would be an infra-temporal millennium—a reign of Christ on earth for a thousand years, previous to the general judgment. Teilhard's theory of progress and evolution, indeed, proposes an optimistic outcome of the evolutionary process—a final consummation

---

*The present essay is reprinted from *Emmanuel,* September, 1967, pp. 364-367.

of collective thought attaining the fullness of human consciousness. Furthermore, this consummation can be achieved, in the opinion of Teilhard, only in conjunction with the driving force of Christian love. But this outcome, supernatural in itself, carries with it the fullness of the natural development of mankind within and through human history itself, previous to Christ's second coming and the general judgment.

On the other hand, the fullness of natural development of mankind is not the earthly paradise envisioned by the Marxists. This is ruled out by the spiritual nature of man and of the spiritual power directing the course of historic development.

The tensions between Teilhard's thought and traditional Catholic thought which have caused concern deal neither with a Chiliastic millennium nor a Marxist paradise. They relate rather to the following questions: (1) Is the optimistic thought of Teilhard compatible with the predictions of Christ and the constant teaching of the Church concerning "the last things?" (2) Is the optimism of Teilhard regarding the world and man compatible with the existence and progress of evil in the world, the malice of voluntary sin, and the expiation and reparation God requires of man?

A review of traditional opinion on the last things will show, I think, that there is no contradiction with Teilhard's thought.

According to tradition, the time of the last day lies hidden in great mystery. However, Catholic Faith believes in six signs to precede the end of the world. To a greater or lesser extent these signs in one way or another are present continuously in three evident conditions in the world which remind men of every generation of the eventual end

Christian Optimism and the Last Things 55

of the world. These comprise, first, evidences in the physical world; secondly, the foreboding presence of the mystery of evil in the world, which must eventually meet with God's judgment; and finally, the persistence of God's goodness to men, despite their wickedness, which is the prelude to His final rewarding of the elect with beatitude at the last judgment.

The first sign refers to the physical world and consists in severe tribulations, such as earthquakes, famines and the like. These were prefigured in a special way by the destruction of Jerusalem, as foretold by Christ in the twenty-fourth chapter of St. Matthew's Gospel.

The second and third signs to precede Christ's second coming relate to the mystery of iniquity in the world: A great falling away from God, which St. Paul calls the great apostasy, and the corresponding rise of many false prophets. In addition, there is the mystery of antichrist, a symbol of the influence of wickedness in the world, described by St. Paul as follows: "Let no one deceive you in any way, for the day of the Lord will not come unless the apostasy comes first, and the man of sin is revealed, the son of perdition, who opposes and is exalted above all that is called God, or that is worshiped, so that he sits in the temple of God and gives himself out as if he were God" (2 Thessalonians 2:3-5).

Finally the last three signs have to do with the mystery of God's goodness. First of all, there is the preaching of the Gospel to the whole world. "And this gospel of the kingdom shall be preached to the whole world" (Matthew 24:14); "...and there shall be one fold and one shepherd" (John 10:17). Necessarily linked to the preceding, and also a prelude to the following is the conversion of the gentiles: the *conversio gentium.* And finally comes the salvation of the Jews, according to St. Paul's words: "For I would not have you ignorant, brethern, of this mystery, lest you be wise in your own conceits, that a partial blindness only has befallen Israel, until the full number of gentiles shall enter, and thus all Israel should be saved, as it is written, 'There will come out of Sion the deliverer and he will turn impiety from Jacob; and this is my covenant with them, when I shall take away their sins.' In view of the Gospel, they are enemies for your sake; but in view of the divine choice, they are most dear for the sake of the fathers. For the gifts and the call of God are without repentance" (Romans 11: 25-29).

"The gifts of God are without repentance." The optimisim of St. Paul, expressed in these words, is the very spirit of Teilhard. His mission was to re-assert Christian conviction in this regard. He does not deny the existence and growth of evil, though some of the phrases in this connection may cause perplexity. In these cases, we must remember that Teilhard's message as such is not concerned with evil in the world—therefore his conceptions here stand open to correction in whatever way necessary—but with the victory of good over evil. In much the same way as Pope John does in his encyclical "Pacem in Terris," he proposes a positive point of view. This does not deny the obstacles that may stand in the way in the fulfillment of their vision. But, of course, those destined to implement the vision must face these problems. In doing so, however, they must not feel that somehow mankind is "trapped" in a world whose ultimate outcome will give victory to the present or future antichristian forces which have been at work since the beginning. No, they are fighting for a world

Christian Optimism and the Last Things 57

that has already mysteriously risen in Christ and to whom the victory has been assured—in time and in eternity. St. Paul made this very clear to the Thessalonians, saying that the Lord Jesus slays the antichrist with the breath of his mouth and the brightness of his coming (Thessalonians 2: 8). This victory is constantly reassured by the expiation and reparation for sin made by the Eucharistic Christ, whose influence and presence spreads over the world the saving remedy for the universal pollution of our worldly atmosphere.

Only the enlightened understanding of this condition will enable mankind to act, to arouse man from the paralysis of fear in the sight of the full-tide of contemporary evil, and to enable him to take evolution in his own hands in the fulfillment of God's own designs—man's complete happiness and God's glory, to be achieved here on earth.

Without this conviction and hope for success, there might be a "strike" in the noosphere. On the other hand, the full consciousness of this conviction, spread abroad, does not preclude the possibility of a break-up of humanity into two segments—those desirous of pushing mankind towards the progress that God intends and those not so willing. One hundred years ago, this possibility was foreseen by Newman—not to mention Augustine over a thousand years ago—who predicted an ultimate division of mankind into believers and unbelievers.

It seems reasonable that such an eventuality might well occur. Nevertheless, it is not necessary to press the distinction between "those who believe in God" and "those who do not" but between those who wish to work for genuine human progress and those who do not.

We may compare Pope John and Teilhard's respective

missions in the twentieth century to the mission of St. John the Baptist, who pointed to the presence of Christ in the world. John was supposed to have been the precursor of Christ's first coming, but Christ was already in the world when he made his great announcement: "Behold the Lamb of God! Behold Him who takes away the sins of the world!" John pointed to the actual presence of Christ in the world previous to the period of his public ministry that was to terminate with his victorious Resurrection in spite of the intervening conflicts with evil. So Teilhard points to the General Resurrection of mankind, with the second coming of Christ at the end of time, but simultaneously reminds us of the actual presence of the Risen Christ in the world, directing it towards its destiny, notwithstanding the intervening conflicts with evil. Before the second coming there must be the "public ministry" of the millennia of human progress, made possible by the consciousness of men of their own possibilities united with Christ and with each other. The great witness to a communistic and secularistic world of the actual presence of Christ in the world is the vitality of Christ's members working together and with all men of good will to establish peace on earth and the happiness of mankind. This is the "millennium" for which every Christian must hope; but, in the broad vision of Teilhard, it can never come unless every Christian helps to "build the earth" with a genuine love for God and for all mankind. Or, in the memorable words of Pope John: "Every believer in this world of ours must be a spark of light, a center of love, a vivifying leaven amidst his fellowmen; and he will be this all the more perfectly the more closely he lives in communion with God and in the intimacy of his own soul."

5.

THE PAROUSIA

In the previous essay we tried to show that in its main themes Teilhard's conception of the Parousia is compatible with traditional doctrine concerning the last things. Now it seems appropriate to sketch out in further detail Teilhard de Chardin's complete view in this understandably important matter.

As a Catholic priest, the famous Jesuit had the greatest faith in the second coming of Christ. Evolution provided him with a springboard from which he proceeded to a broad vision of the Parousia as foretold in Christian Revelation. In and through evolution, as he understood and interpreted it, he hoped to reconcile science with the data of faith. How?

Teilhard dismisses any Darwinian conception of evolution. Darwin's evolution was mechanistic and unguided. If Darwin's point of view were correct, pessimism concerning man's future in the course of evolution would be in order. Sartre would be correct then in expounding a theory that life is utterly absurd and meaningless. This is not the way that Teilhard envisions evolution. Evolution has meaning. It is guided. It is finalistic and eschatological. Optimism is the keynote.

According to Teilhard, evolution proceeds both from an attraction from on high and from a thrust from below. This evolution is continual and has a convergent direction—ever onward and upward. When under the direction of Christ the forces of natural evolution converge with the forces of the supernatural world, the world will have reached the purpose of its existence and its growth, and the Parousia will take place.

Here is where a difficulty arises. In the traditional vision of the Last Things, Christ's second coming is to be immediately preceded by catastrophic events. In Teilhard's view, these catastrophic events are spread out indefinitely according to his long-range view of evolutionism's progress, growth, and conflict (both in the natural and supernatural orders). According to the more traditional view, the Parousia will be an event of a purely catastrophic nature. It may come about at any moment in history, irrespective of any definite state of mankind. Not so Teilhard. The world and mankind must be prepared: "Why should we not assume, in accordance with the latest scientific view of mankind in a state of anthropogenesis, that the parousiac spark can, of physical and organic necessity, only be kindled between heaven and a mankind which has biologically reached a certain critical evolutionary point of collective maturity." (FM, 267) In other words, the second coming of Christ must be preceded and prepared by a long process of human development, which itself has carried on from the whole of earlier evolutions. For Teilhard, this idea or view, is perfectly analogous with the mystery of the first Christmas, which "could not have operated (as is universally agreed) except between heaven and earth that

The Parousia

was socially, politically, and psychologically ready to receive Jesus." (FM, 267)

This "revised" approach seems to present no theological or traditional difficulty for Teilhard—and he hopes no serious difficulty for anyone. For: "...it seems to me certain, on the other hand, that by the very fact of making this simple readjustment in our 'eschatological' vision we shall have performed an operation having incalculable consequences. For if truly, in order that the Kingdom of God may come (in order that the Pleroma may close in upon the fullness), it is necessary, as an essential physical condition, that the human earth should already have attained the natural completion of its evolutionary growth, then it must mean that the ultra-human perfection which Neohumanism envisages for Evolution will coincide in concrete terms with the growing of the Incarnation awaited by all Christians." (FM, 268)

Are we therefore to imply that evolution will ultimately cause the Parousia to arrive? No. This would be a misunderstanding of Teilhard. For he admits the gulf between the present world and the beyond-this-world. There are two worlds. And thus we must distinguish, as does Teilhard, two convergences, two separate, evolutionary processes: one is cosmic (natural)—the other is Christic (supernatural). A natural world evolves to a supernatural world? No! But by the direction of Christ, the author of both natural and supernatural evolution, at a certain point there will be a convergence of the two movements. It will be so only because of the gratuitous direction of Christ who assumed the center of our natural world when He took flesh and became part of the evolutionary current for which He Himself is responsible. Henri de Lubac, in his book on

Teilhard: The Man and His Meaning (p. 125)[1] clearly states this: "No sort of 'cosmic convergence' then, would suffice to produce the 'parousiac spark.' No 'point of human maturation' can by itself release the 'point of Christic parousia.'"

It is here we come upon the "Omega Point" concept of Teilhard—it is the final, converging point of the material and spiritual world. Teilhard's vision of the world is entirely orientated toward the terminus and fulfillment actually toward Christ who shall be all in all. "The Incarnation is a renewal and a restoration of all the forces and powers of the universe. Christ is the instrument, the center, the end of all animate and material creation. By Him all things are created, sanctified and made alive. This is the constant and customary teaching of St. John and St. Paul (the most 'cosmic' of the sacred writers)." (FM, 304) *In Him we live, move, and have our being* (Acts 17:28). Teilhard joins the necessarily divergent worlds of matter and spirit to a convergent finale in Christ.

This idea of one fulfillment, one terminus, is not so difficult to appreciate. For in the *Hymn of the Universe,* Teilhard simply states: "The world can no more have two summits of fulfillment than a circumference can have two centers." (HU, 149) Christ is not all things—pantheistically speaking—but He is the one true center of the whole material universe. In the *Phenomenon of Man,* Teilhard explains: "Thus it would be mistaken to represent Omega to ourselves simply as a center born of the fusion of elements which it collects, or annihilating them in itself. By its structure Omega, in its ultimate principle, can only

---

[1] Henri de Lubac, *Teilhard de Chardin: The Man and His Meaning.* (New York: Hawthorne Books, Inc., 1965), p. 125.

be a distinct center radiating at the core of a system of centers; a grouping in which personalization of the all and personalizations of the elements reach their maximum, simultaneously and without merging, under the influence of a supremely autonomous focus of union." (PM, 262-263) And this central, autonomous focal point, is exactly what Teilhard means by the expression: Omega Point. Ever since Christ was born, when He finished His own growth, died, and rose again, everything has continued to grow—to move. "Christ has not yet completed His own forming...in the pursuance of this engendering is situated the ultimate spring of all created activity...Christ is the Fulfillment even of the natural evolution of beings." (FM, 305)

As a scientist, Teilhard immerses himself in the material world. But he dedicated himself essentially to a good beyond this world. In a letter of January, 1917, we have his own views on the world and how it leads him to the other world: "For me the real earth is that chosen part of the universe still almost everywhere dispersed, and in the course of slow separation, but which is gradually taking on body in the form of Christ."[2] We can't help but be led to the final point of juncture with Christ. For the very evolutionary drive—onward to the Omega Point—is a magnetic drive of the Divinity: "The universality of your divine magnetism and the intrinsic value of our human undertakings: this, My God, is the twofold truth you have shown me, and I am burning to spread abroad the knowledge of it and to bring it fully into effect." (HU, 151)

Anyone who wishes to wander about in the excitement of this final union of the two worlds—a convergent mix-

---

[2] From a letter, January 9, 1917, quoted by de Lubac, *op. cit.,* p. 123.

ture where Christ will be the terminus of union—will no doubt fancy premonitions of pantheism in this finalistic, eschatological ending to evolution as Teilhard envisages it. Some, indeed, have accused Teilhard of pantheism. But to assuage the error and assure the critics, Teilhard himself anticipated the accusation in the *Phenomenon of Man.* In this work Teilhard explains a favorite point of his—that union differentiates. In any domain (biological, i.e., cells of a body; sociological, i.e., members of a society) we see that in every organized whole, the parts perfect themselves and fulfill themselves. "Through neglect of this universal rule many a system of pantheism has led us astray to the cult of the great All in which individuals were supposed to be merged like a drop in the ocean or like a dissolving grain of salt. Applied to the case of the summation of consciousness, the law of union rids us of this perilous and recurrent illusion. No, following the confluent orbits of their centers, the grains of consciousness do not tend to lose their outlines and blend but, on the contrary, to accentuate the depth and incommunicability of their egos....

"Thus under the influence of these two factors—the essential immiscibility of consciousness, and the natural mechanism of all unification—the only fashion in which we could correctly express the final state of a world undergoing psychical concentration would be as a system whose unity coincides with a paroxism of harmonized complexity." (PM, 262)

But what have evolution, Omega Point, final union of two worlds, and the like, to do with the Parousia? For Teilhard de Chardin, evolution and all the other abovementioned ideas, are stepping stones and roadsigns to the final coming of Christ in the Parousia. Evolution, for

Teilhard, will bring all things to end up at a definite point. The history of the universe, as read from the data of evolution, means growth, and according to Teilhard, this growth must be irreversible and its results everlasting.[3] The whole idea of evolution leads one to ultimately declare life is to go on forever somehow. And for the Christian, this will be at the second coming. The morbid views of the existentialism of a Sartre are unfounded—"the great enigma presented to our minds by the phenomenon of man is not so much how life could ever have been kindled on earth as how it could ever be extinguished on earth without finding some continuance elsewhere. For once life has become reflective consciousness, it cannot in fact accept utter extinction without biologically contradicting itself." (HU, 105)

"Let us admit this frankly once and for all: what most discredits faith in progress in the eyes of men today, over and above its reticences and its helplessness in meeting the cry of the 'last days of the human species,' is the unfortunate tendency still shown by its adepts to distort into pitiful millinarianisms all that is most valid and most noble in our now permanently awakened expectation of the future appearance of some form of 'ultra-humanity.' An era of abundance and euphoria—a Golden Age—is, they suggest, all that evolution could hold in reserve for us. And it is but right that our hearts should sink at the thought of so 'bourgeois' an ideal." (HU, 109) No, man is redeemed to immortality with the Creator. He is soul and body both, not only a bundle of highly organized cells and nerve

---

[3] Oliver Rabut, O.P., *Teilhard de Chardin: A Critical Study*. (New York: Sheed and Ward, 1961), p. 116.

tissues. This onward groping evidenced in the evolution of life can lead to only one condition: unity with the center of centers, the Omega Point, which will be consummated as the Pleroma and the Parousia will occur.

But exactly what will be the manner in which the parousiac spark will ignite? How will the final outcome take place? In what way does Teilhard envision that the unique process of assimilation and synthesis, of segregation and aggregation pursued from the beginning of time will come to an end? The presence of Christ, which has been silently accruing in all things, will suddenly be revealed— "...like a flash of lightning amid the storm-clouds of a slowly consecrated world. The trumpets of the angels are but a weak symbol. It is in the grip of the most powerful organic attraction conceivable (the force which held the universe together) that the monads will pour into that place whither they are irrevocably destined by the total maturing of all things and the implacable irreversibility of the whole history of the world." (FM, 307) In the *Divine Milieu* Teilhard further describes this 'flash of light': "Breaking through all the barriers within which the veil of matter and the water-tightness of souls have seemingly kept it confined, it will invade the face of the earth. And, under the finally-liberated action of the true affinities of being the spiritual atoms of the world will be borne along by a force generated by the powers of cohesion proper to the universe itself, and will occupy, whether within Christ or without Christ, the place of happiness or pain designated for them by the living structure of the Pleroma....Like lightning, like a conflagration, like a flood, the attraction exerted by the Son of Man will lay hold of all the whirling elements in the universe so as to reunite them or subject them to His body." (DM, 150-151)

The Parousia

Such will be the consummation of "the divine milieu." But when will this happen? Is it possible to foresee, in the footsteps of the earth's evolution when this will all take place? It would seem vain to speculate—all we can do is to expect it. We shall never know all that the Incarnation still expects of the world with all its potentialities. But all we must do is hope and strongly grip the wonderful evolving process—the growing process of the unity of mankind.

Teilhard lived this hope and then he strove to awaken and maintain a sense of expectation—even a passionate, active hope in the coming of Christ as foretold in revelation and as evidenced in the unifying element of evolution. "Expectation—anxious, collective and operative expectation of an end of this world,...—that is perhaps the supreme Christian function and the most distinctive characteristic of our religion." (DM, 151)

Every man desires happiness to a perfect degree. He hungers, from the very beginning, for immortal life. If there were no after-life, no resurrection, or second coming, this life would be certainly absurd and meaningless. For us, as Christians, Revelation brings assurance of another life. Teilhard invites non-Christians and even atheists, who only believe in this world and the data of scientific evolution, to come to our own saving hope. They too can perceive, as he did, the finalistic surge of evolution which will eventually lead to a summit. If evolution were non-directive, it would be futile, seemingly organized but chaotic self-destruction. If this evolution, this growing world has direction—it can lead all in its path to the very summit which will be Christ—it will lead all, believers and non-believers, back to the Creator. Creation has purpose— and as a result the only definitive world for Teilhard is

Christ. For this world will culminate to Christ-Omega, in Whom the Pleroma is to be consummated on the day of the Second Coming—the "Parousia."

Thus the world becomes a one-way road to Christ. His keen sense of the ultimate goal of the world's restoration in Christ enflamed Teilhard with a mystic reverence for the world. This inspired him to write this beautiful prayer, with which he ended his spiritual testament, *The Divine Milieu.*

"Jerusalem, lift up your head. Look at the immense crowds of those who build and those who seek. All over the world men are toiling—in laboratories, in studios, in deserts, in factories, in the vast social crucible. The ferment that is taking place by their instrumentality in art and science and thought is happening for your sake. Open, then, your arms and your heart, like Christ your Lord, and welcome the waters, the flood and the sap of humanity. Accept it, this sap, for, without its baptism, you will wither, without desire, like a flower out of water; and tend it, since, without your sun it will disperse itself wildly in sterile shoots....

"Now the earth can certainly clasp me in her giant arms. She can swell me with her life, or take me back into her dust. She can deck herself out for me with every charm, with every horror, with every mystery. She can intoxicate me with her perfume of tangibility and unity. She can cast me to my knees in expectation of what is maturing in her breast.

"But her enchantment can no longer do me harm, since she has become for me, over and above herself, the body of him who is and of him who is coming—The Divine Milieu." (DM, 154-155)

6.

TEILHARD AND THE FRANCISCAN SCHOOL

Raise me up, then, matter, to those heights, through struggle and separation and death; raise me up until, at long last, it becomes possible for me in perfect chastity to embrace the universe. (HU, 70)

Previous essays have compared some aspects of the thought of Teilhard with those of St. Thomas Aquinas. Now it seems appropriate to contrast Teilhard with the Franciscan school of philosophy, and especially with St. Bonaventure and with Duns Scotus. There are two points of similarity that should be brought out here, viz., the conception of matter and the primacy of Christ.

The Dynamic Conception of Matter

We must place our discussion of matter in an historical perspective. Man's ideas about matter have not been static, but rather they have been subject to continual development. What a philosopher of the thirteenth century wrote about matter was conditioned by thirteenth century knowledge of science. We can transplant his thought into the intellectual environment of the twentieth century only by taking into account changes in the fundamental concepts of science during the intervening years.

The point to be made here is that St. Bonaventure spoke of matter in a thirteenth century intellectual environment quite distant in scientific progress from the twentieth century intellectual environment of Teilhard de Chardin. With this in mind we can begin our study.

First of all, we should trace briefly St. Bonaventure's *weltanschauung* or world-view.

It is typical of the Seraphic Doctor to see traces of the Trinity everywhere in creation. In this way all creation is filled with intelligible likenesses leading us to God. "The created world," St. Bonaventure says, "is like a book in which the creative Trinity shines forth, is represented, and is read..." (*Breviloquium,* II, 12). When the understanding is enlightened by faith, the book of nature becomes a resplendent path leading us to God. Thus, St. Bonaventure integrates reason and faith. The metaphysician, he says, proceeds from the consideration of created, particular substance to the uncreated and universal substance not in the pantheistic sense, of course, and so, in so far as he deals with the originating Principle of all things, he is akin to the natural philosopher (or, in modern terminology, the physicist), who also considers the origin of things. But Bonaventure insists that the metaphysician, unlike the mere physicist, must see beyond matter in his consideration of the universe. He must consider God, the Supreme Being, as the exemplary cause of all things. Nor can he stop here. He must take into account, not only that God is the exemplary cause of all things, but that the *medium* of creation, the express image of the Father and the exemplar of all creatures, is the Divine Word, Who became man in Christ. Precisely as a philosopher he cannot come to a certain knowledge of the Word, it is true; but then if he is content to be a mere philosopher, he will fall into error: he must, enlightened by faith, proceed beyond mere philosophy and realize that the Divine Word is exemplary Cause of all things. In this sense Christ becomes the *medium* not only of theology but also of philosophy. In fact, Christian philosophy means precisely this: to know that everything comes from God and returns back to God through the *medium* which is Christ, the Word Incarnate. This emphasis of the place of Christ in Bonaventure's vision has caused his commentators to characterize his philosophy as Christocentric.

Regarding the material world, St. Bonaventure adopts the metaphysics of light taught at Oxford by Robert Grosseteste and Roger Bacon. According to them, all bodies are composed of matter and the basic form of light. Light is not simply an accidental form of bodies but the noblest of all substantial bodily forms. It is the universal active principle in bodies, giving them their basic energy and activity. Other substantial forms perfect matter subsequent to this form.

In itself the form of light is imperceptible. Visible light is not the form itself but simply a striking manifestation of it. God is pure light, dwelling in light inaccessible (I Timothy 6:16). Light in the created universe is a participation in God's light. All the activities of bodies, plants, animals, and men stem from the basic energy of light. Even sensible knowledge (vision) takes place through light; and on a higher level, through a higher energy of light—illumination—intellectual knowledge occurs. This doctrine enables St. Bonaventure to stress the analogy between the universe and God and the beauty of creatures as a mirror of the divine beauty.

For Teilhard, too, matter is sacred. It is a part of a Christocentric universe which manifests God. In *The Divine Milieu* Teilhard writes:

> ...by virtue of the Creation and, still more, of the Incarnation, *nothing* here below is *profane* for those who know how to see. On the contrary, everything is sacred to those capable of distinguishing that portion of chosen being which is subject to attraction of Christ in the process of consummation. (DM, 66)

Attached to this sacredness of matter is a certain spiritual power. In *The Hymn of the Universe* Teilhard addresses himself to matter: "I acclaim you as the divine milieu, charged with creative power, as the ocean stirred by the Spirit, as the clay molded and infused with life by the incarnate Word." (HU, 70) Teilhard believed in these words because he acknowledged deeply the growth of life on earth.

We have suggested in previous essays that the "creative power" inherent in matter is due to God's presence. For Teilhard, the creative power of God manifests itself through various forms of energy, and especially by "radial" energy, which he sometimes calls the "within" of things. The question arises, what is the primordial or most fundamental manifestation of God's power, acting from within His creation? Teilhard's answer to this question is linked, with modern scientific conceptions, to his view of matter as energy and light.

In *The Phenomenon of Man,* Teilhard presents three faces of matter: plurality (or radically particulate), unity (or essentially related), and energy (or prodigously active). (PM, 40)

It is precisely the last of these three faces, that is, energy, that we intend to further discuss.

To begin with, Teilhard says that—

Energy is the measure of that which passes from one atom to another in the course of their transformations. A unifying power, then, but also, because the atom appears to become enriched or exhausted in the course of the exchange, the expression of structure. (PM, 42)

Teilhard goes on to explain that—

From the aspect of energy, renewed by radioactive phenomena, material corpuscles may now be treated as transient reservoirs of concentrated power. Though never found in a state of purity, but always more or less granulated (even in light), energy nowadays represents for science the most primitive form of universal stuff. (PM, 42)

With modern scientists, Teilhard believes that energy is the most primitive form of universal stuff. What is noteworthy for our purposes is Teilhard's reference to light. We have seen how light played an important role for St. Bonaventure in his concept of matter. Continuing his discussion on matter in *The Phenomenon of Man,* Teilhard mentions *luminosity* in matter.

As seen in its central portion, which is the most distinct, the evolution of matter, in current theory, comes back to the gradual building up by growing complication of the various elements recognized by physical chemistry. To begin with, at the very bottom there is a still unresolved simplicity, luminous in nature and not to be defined in terms of figures. (PM, 47)

In his other works Teilhard returns to the theme of *luminosity* in nature, but with an applied and analogous meaning. Like St. Bonaventure, he uses analogies and comparisons to rise from his more perfected knowledge of light to a higher order. In *The Hymn of the Universe,* for instance, Teilhard compares the world to a crystal lamp illumined from within by the light of Christ. This image leads to another central theme in Teilhard: *diaphany.* This is a Greek word which means to "appear through." This term in Teilhard refers to the appearing of God through matter, to the shining of Christ through the cosmos. For those who can see, Christ shines in a diaphany, through the cosmos and in matter.

Teilhard understands the divine diaphany as dynamic. God imparts light energy to matter which causes it to rise to fulfillment "...under the influence of this inner light which penetrated it, its fibers were stretched to breaking point and all the energies within them were strained to the utmost." (HU, 48)

For Teilhard, matter from the beginning took on an evolutionary goal. God imparted light energy to matter which caused it to rise to fulfillment. The final state of matter, diaphanous in nature, will be "christification," after the process of Christogenesis has been completed at the end of time. This "divinization" of matter occurs because of its dynamic aspect of energy, which is luminous in nature. Thus, light is simultaneously the first expression of God's power, or diaphany; a symbol of Christ; and an anticipation of "the new heavens and a new earth" at the end of time.

St. Bonaventure is similar to Teilhard in the use of

Teilhard and the Franciscan School

images to express the presence of God in the universe. The world is a mirror that reflects God.[1] It is a stained glass window through which the divine light shines in multicolored variety.[2] It is a book in which we read the wisdom of God. The world is a ladder on which we climb to God.[3]

The point we wish to make is not so much the point of Bonaventure using images as Teilhard but that both Bonaventure and Teilhard see the material universe as the manifestation of God's presence and power in the world. Commentators point out that for Bonaventure God shines through the material world in His power, wisdom and goodness. We must contemplate God not only *through* creatures but also *in* creatures: He is in the world in His essence, power and presence.

Such an interest was typical of the Franciscan spirit. Cousins notes that they were the forerunners of modern empirical science. Accordingly,

> It is not surprising then, that out of the empirical scientific tradition, there should arise a man like Teilhard, who discovers in the material world the very diaphany of Christ that inspired the medieval Franciscans to explore the world of matter.[4]

The Incarnation for St. Bonaventure was the most perfect of all God's works and like Teilhard he sees in matter a tendency pointing to the Incarnation.[5]

---

[1] St. Bonaventure, *Itinerarium Mentis In Deum.* I, 9.
[2] St. Bonaventure, *Collationes In Hexaemeron.* XII, 14.
[3] St. Bonaventure, *Breviloquium.* II, II, 2. See also *Itinerarium.*
[4] Michael D. Meilach, *There Shall Be One Christ, Essays on Teilhard.* (New York: St. Bonaventure, 1968), p. 11.
[5] St. Bonaventure, *Breviloquium.* IV, 4, 4.

The natural tendency in matter is so ordained to intellectual causes that the generation is in no way perfect unless the rational soul be united to the material body. By similar reasoning, therefore we come to the conclusion that the highest and noblest perfection can exist in this world only if a nature in which there are intellectual causes, and a nature in which there are seminal causes, and a nature in which there are the ideal causes are simultaneously combined in the unity of one person, as was done in the Incarnation of the Son of God....

He is the Alpha and the Omega, that is, He was begotten in the beginning and before all time but became Incarnate in the fulness of time.[6]

Thus the Incarnation renders the cosmos sacramental. This is indeed fortunate for today when the cosmos is a major part of our cultural experience. Man needs a spirituality that emphasizes the universe and explores the spiritual power of matter as indicative of God's presence. Such a spirituality is proper both to Teilhard and to St. Bonaventure. In Teilhard's thought, the initial creative power of God first manifests itself in energy and inner light, which gives rise to evolution. St. Bonaventure was also very much aware of the creative power of God in nature, as is clear from his interpretation, adopted from St. Augustine, of original matter. He held that, although God could have completed the world of bodies immediately, He preferred to produce it at first in an imperfect state and in an incomplete form, so that matter might rise towards God, the outcry, as it were, and the appeal of its very

---

6 St. Bonaventure, *De Reductione Artium Ad Theolgiam.* 20.

imperfection.[7] St. Bonaventure was speaking here of matter "rising toward God" in reference to the six days of creation. Teilhard of course infers that the "rise towards God" continues on after the six days. But the uniqueness and the similarity of these two men is that for both matter evolved onwards, became more and more complex. There is a note of development or evolution. There is a difference only in the question of duration. For Teilhard it is going on; for St. Bonaventure this rise of matter has already taken place.

For St. Bonaventure, as for Teilhard, there was indeed a sort of universal expectation of God in all things. Gilson explains that Bonaventure admits that matter was created by God clothed with a certain form (light), but that this form was not a complete form and that it did not confer upon corporeal nature its complete being. This solution has for him the advantage not only of making more intelligible the temporal development of creation in six days, but also implanting in the very heart of things a sort of universal expectation of God.[8]

Now, the original form of light in St. Bonaventure seems to correspond to Teilhard's third face in matter—luminous energy which is the first "within" of things. The parallel between the two thinkers on matter is now clear. For both men, matter embodies a certain dynamic aspect. St. Bonaventure's dynamic aspect of matter was light; for Teilhard, it was luminous energy, which is the first (created) "within" of material reality. For both men, matter tends to rise towards its fulfillment in God. Just as the first "within"

---

7 E. Gilson, *The Philosophy of St. Bonaventure*. (Paterson, N.J.: St. Anthony, 1965), p. 273.
8 *Ibid.*, p. 284.

of luminous energy actuates matter for Teilhard, so the form of light is the fundamental manifestation of God for St. Bonaventure.

This is the first point of similarity between Teilhard and the Franciscan School. Next we must study the question of the primacy of Christ.

The Primacy of Christ

As previously stated, St. Bonaventure puts Christ in the center of all philosophical and theological speculation. He is the "Medium omnium scientiarum." Faithful to this spirit, the Franciscan Duns Scotus emphasized "the primacy of Christ" in creation. Teilhard's thought is aligned with this tradition. In his vision, the entire creation centers upon Christ as its natural crowning point, so that the order of creation is incomplete without Him. Like Scotus, Teilhard bases himself upon St. Paul. St. Francis de Sales, Newman, and Scheeben have also defended this position.

In their perspective, Jesus Christ is held to be the goal and the crowning-point not only of the supernatural but also of the natural order. Right from the beginning, and quite independently of the fall of man into sin, the whole creation was planned with the God-Man in view. Even if man had not sinned, the Word would have become man; for Christ is the supreme revelation of God in this world and the masterpiece of God's creation.

Teilhard transferred this perspective to an evolving world, hoping to establish a link between the God-Man and evolution. And he thought that the link should be more than an external, juridical connection. If Teilhard's contribution was original, it is because he stated the old problem of the place of Christ in God's plan for the world in a new way.

Teilhard insisted that despite the repeated affirmation of St. Paul and the Greek fathers, theologians for the most part have considered the universal power of Christ over creation from an extrinsic and juridical point of view. He found a decided difference in Duns Scotus. In Scotian theology the primary motive of the Incarnation is not to counteract the effects of sin in the world, either original or personal, but the glorification of the God-Man as the greatest act of love, the supreme reason and the first intention of the divine Will. This is similar to Teilhard's idea. God's purpose in creating is to unite all reality— material and spiritual, natural and supernatural, divine and human—in the Person of the Incarnate Word. But in Teilhard's viewpoint, this vision shared by Duns Scotus must be seen in the context of evolution and cosmogenesis, and it is this context which forces him to shift his emphasis in explaining his thought.

Perhaps this will become clear if we state three possible positions which one might hold concerning the Creation, Incarnation, and Redemption. To prevent all misunderstanding, let it be stated clearly that Catholic Faith teaches three things, which must be sustained in any case. First, creation is gratuitous. Secondly, in the present order of things, God became man to save mankind from sin. Thirdly, and again in the actual economy of salvation, Christ holds the primacy. In the words of St. Paul: "In Him all things hold together." "In all things He has the first place" (Colossians 1:18).

The first position is that of St. Thomas, who stresses the redemption and puts it in first place in his thought.

To him, it is quite conceivable, in the abstract, to consider creation without redemption and incarnation, but not the Incarnation without the Redemption. The second point of view is that of Duns Scotus, who cannot conceive the Creation without the Incarnation, but who can conceive the Incarnation without the Redemption (in the supposition there has been no sin). Thus the Incarnation holds first place in his thought. Teilhard's way of thinking differs from both of the preceding, for he refuses to separate the Creation, even in thought, from the Incarnation and Redemption. Thus he conforms his speculation to the actual order of things. As he sees it, in any supposition, God creates in order to lift up His creation to Himself by a gradual process and direct it from within to its fulfillment of union with God, and He does this decisively by becoming man. In this third position, however, Teilhard sees evolution as an appropriate (if not necessary) means. As Father Mooney has pointed out, it is regrettable that Teilhard so emphasizes evolution as a natural process that he sometimes seems to neglect the gratuitousness of creation on the one hand, and the tragedy of sin on the other. His vision really becomes much more complete if natural evolution is seen as occurring within the framework of a universe, not only to be lifted up, but to be redeemed. Then, against the background of evolution, the redemptive work of Christ as Alpha (in His divine Person) and as Omega (as God Incarnate) takes on a triple role: to hold all creation together, to move it towards its goal by personally immersing Himself in it, and to overcome by His Love the resistance and malice of those who oppose His divine plan.

If evolution could be seen in this perspective (Teilhard

was convinced), contemporary man would be brought to understand the secret that has been hidden from the foundation of the world—the breadth and length and height and depth of the love of Christ for mankind. What is the conclusion to be drawn from Teilhard's perspective? It is this. It is time for mankind (through Christianity) to become conscious of the meaning of evolution: God's love for man in Christ. In previous centuries, the application of Christian revelation shed light on a number of truths known by reason. Thus, the finite nature of the universe was explained by creation, i.e., a free act of love on the part of God. The power of evil in the world was explained by man's sinfulness from the beginning, which is overcome by God's grace (God's free gift of Himself to man) in Christ. Now the mystery of the growth and direction of human history and evolution is explained by the controlling power of Christ over the world's destiny, notwithstanding human malice. This destiny, freely and intelligently recognized by man come of age, is the glorious triumph of God's plan of universal redemption for the whole human race. No other possible conclusion is open: God has united Himself to us, in order to unite mankind to Him—through redemption, through His whole directive influence on the evolutionary and historical process, which must terminate in Christ.

The perspective of Teilhard is *new* only in the sense that he presents it from a *scientific* point of view. At least such is his claim, yet admitting that in its final prospect an act of faith is involved. On the other hand, the same vista enjoyed by Teilhard is *not* new if considered from a *theological* point of view. Perhaps there is no better proof of this than the following statement of Pope Paul VI:

"...the meaning and direction of history (is) not a mere succession of human vicissitudes within the blind and inescapable play of natural and cosmic becoming, but rather an evolutionary process which man is undergoing and which we *believe* to be guided by a dominant Thought, leading all things towards a possible and free result which is salvation (cf. Romans 8:28). (Discourse of May 13, 1970, italics added.)

Or, again, in another passage, the same Holy Father pointed out that, in evaluating the history of the world and of man, the Church "finds a chain of events through which there runs an *impulse* leading to and centering in Christ."[9]

---

[9] Pope Paul VI, *The Church.* (Boston: St. Paul's Editions, 1967), p. 33.

7.

TEILHARD AND MODERN THOUGHT

Teilhard de Chardin once complained that he was living in two different worlds: one was a world shared with members of the Catholic Faith, the other the world of his scientist friends, who often were unbelievers. The question arises: How similar were his views to those of the philosopher scientists of his time? The answer does not seem difficult to give. John MacQuarrie in *Studies in Christian Existentialism* locates Teilhard's position as follows:

> As far as his dynamic world-view is concerned, Teilhard stands in the closest affinity with the process philosophies, and indeed he says nothing of importance that has not already been said—less picturesquely, perhaps, but often with more philosophical rigor —by such thinkers as Samuel Alexander and A.N. Whitehead.[1]

The process philosophy of Whitehead holds that it is the nature of reality to move forward, to progress. His humanistic reflections were colored and reinforced by the concept of evolution, an evolution that is at the same time

---

[1] John MacQuarrie, *Studies in Christian Existentialism.* (Philadelphia: Westminster Press, 1965), p. 187.

biological, sociological, and intellectual. Teilhard was also convinced of generalized evolution and spoke of one gigantic process, a process of becoming, of attaining complexity and existence. Teilhard views phenomenon as in an evolving process having specific direction and pattern. Both Whitehead and Teilhard decry the static-concept theory of the universe. Whitehead goes a step further. He states that—

> Enduring things are...the outcome of a temporal process;...only if you take material to be fundamental, this property of endurance is an arbitrary fact at the base of the order of nature; but if you take organism to be fundamental, this property is the result of evolution.[2]

Teilhard reiterates and intensifies this: the universe is in movement; nothing, not even the soul of man, escapes this universal law. (FM, 12-13)

Concerning the conditions and advancement of this obvious evolution, for so they regard it, Teilhard concentrates on the development of man. He says that what is in store for man is a global unity of mankind's noetic organization, in love, goodwill and full cooperation, with personal integration and internal harmony and subsequent increasing knowledge. Whitehead talks of an "upward" trend in evolution. "If the choice be happy, evolution has taken an upward trend....The material universe has contained itself, and perhaps still contains, some mysterious impulse for its energy to run upwards...with reason as the selective

---

[2] *The Philosophy of Alfred North Whitehead,* edited by Paul A. Schilipp. (New York: Tudor Publishing Co., 1951), p. 96.

Teilhard and Modern Thought

agency."³ Teilhard calls this "mysterious impulse" the "within" of matter, which is nothing else than God's creative power, variously manifested.

Teilhard and Whitehead were scientistis Teilhard a paleontologist; Whitehead a mathematician. In contrast to most scientists, they met head-on the problem of mind and matter. This is what Teilhard in *The Phenomenon of Man* says about the problem:

> To connect the two energies, of the body and the soul, in a coherent manner: science has provisionally decided to ignore the question, and it would be very convenient for us to do the same. Unfortunately, or fortunately, caught up as we are here in the logic of a system where the "within" of things has just as much or even more value than their "without," we collide with the difficulty head-on. It is impossible to avoid the clash: we must advance. (PM, 62)

Very clearly Teilhard points out the quarrel between materialists and the spiritualists that is seemingly insoluable since the two groups are on different levels. Teilhard, instead, is convinced that the two points of view can be reconciled and brought to agreement. His answer is to talk of the "within" and the "without" of matter, not matter and spirit. He always speaks, then, of the universe as necessarily having "a double aspect to its structure" in which the "without" is co-extensive with the "within." (PM, 53-56)

---

3 Alfred North Whitehead, *The Function of Reason.* (Boston: Beacon Press, 1958), pp. 19, 24.

Concerning dualism, MacQuarrie again gives us the relationship between Teilhard and Whitehead:

> The denial of dualism and the correlation of physical and mental phenomena are also in Alexander, but perhaps the closest parallel to Teilhard's way of expressing it is found in Whitehead's doctrine of the bipolarity of actual entities. According to this doctrine, all actual entities from God down to the veriest 'puff of existence' have both a mental and a physical pole.... (*op. cit.,* p. 187)

Whitehead blames Descartes for all the trouble about mind and matter. It all goes back to the problem of the bridge in which Descartes posited an opposition of mind and matter. This is Whitehead's answer to the problem. It closely parallels that of Teilhard.

> The effect of this sharp division between nature and life has poisoned all subsequent philosophy. Even when the coordinate existence of the two types of actualities is abandoned, there is no proper fusion of the two in most modern schools of thought. For some, nature is mere appearance and mind is the sole reality and mind is an epiphenomenon. Here the phrases "mere appearance" and "epiphenomenon" obviously carry the implication of slight importance for the understanding of the final nature of things.
>
> The doctrine that I am maintaining is that neither physical nature nor life can be understood unless we fuse them together as essential factors in the composition of "really real" things whose interconnections and individual characters constitute the universe.[4]

---

4 *Modes of Thought,* as quoted in Schilipp, *op. cit.,* pp. 266-267.

In his philosophy Whitehead so construed his basic conceptions to be so inclusive in scope as to overcome the classical dualisms of metaphysics. Besides mind and matter he overcame in the process: the dualities of God and the World, permanence and transience, causality and teleology, atomism and continuity, sensation and emotion, internal and external relations, and subject and object. Whitehead's term for this duality is "bifurcation." Whitehead is the avowed enemy of it, but, as Lowe states, "in his zeal he overstates his case."[5]

A logical conclusion to non-duality is Panpsychism — i.e., that all reality has some degree of consciousness. It is here, too, that commentators feel that Teilhard overstates the case. Perhaps his idea would be more acceptable if put in the following way. The creative power of God, which was at the heart of the universe even in its initial simplicity, imparts all the energy necessary to account for the emergence of the various forms that will eventually be manifested in an ever more impressive display of conscious direction and participation by evolving species.

This is how Whitehead speaks of the mergence of mind in his evolutionary process in *Modes of Thought:*

> In so far as conceptual mentality does not intervene, the grand patterns pervading the environment are passed on with the inherited modes of adjustment. Here we find the patterns of activity studied by the physicists and chemists. Mentality is merely latent in all these occasions as thus studied. In the case of inorganic nature any sporadic flashes are inoperative so far as our powers of discernment are concerned.

---

[5] *Ibid.,* p. 85.

> The lowest stages of effective mentality, controlled by the inheritance of physical pattern, involves the faint direction of emphasis by unconscious ideal aim. The various examples of the higher forms of life exhibit the variety of grades of effectiveness of mentality. In the social habits of animals there is evidence of flashes of mentality in the past which have degenerated into physical habits. Finally in the higher mammals and more particularly in mankind, we have clear evidence of mentality habitually effective. In our own experience, our knowledge consciously entertained and systematized can only mean such mentality, directly observed.[6]

In other words, Whitehead believes that there is a successive improvement of mental activity in all things from inorganic matter to man himself.

Teilhard expresses, somewhat bluntly, the same idea. He says the living world consists intrinsically of consciousness clothed in flesh, the result of a gigantic ramification of the spirit. That is to say, the Creating Spirit (God) clothes the various kinds of matter with ascending degrees of awareness, according to the complexity of their structure.

Previously mentioned was the "mysterious impulse" of Whitehead and now the "ramification of the Spirit" of Teilhard. Both philosophers seem to be talking about the same thing. They realize there is something inside everything that makes everything more complex and more conscious. Teilhard would say that there is in the center of matter something which "systematically reaches up-

---

6 *Ibid.,* p. 257.

ward." Whitehead would say that there is a basic constituent of every existing thing (organism) whose intensity of life is of different degrees, and that evolution is an evolution of organisms of ever increasing organization. With more organization comes a greater participation in consciousness. This is exactly identical to Teilhard's law of recurrence—the law of complexity-consciousness: "The degree of concentration of consciousness," states Teilhard in *The Phenomenon of Man,* "varies in inverse ratio to the simplicity of the material compound lined by it." Or, much more clearly identified with Whitehead: "A consciousness (that is) much more perfected according as it lines a richer and better organized material edifice. (PM, 60)

In all this both Teilhard and Whitehead are in agreement in rejecting any mechanistic conception of the universe. Whitehead writes clearly that—

...a thoroughgoing evolutionary philosophy is inconsistent with (mechanistic) materialism. The aboriginal stuff, or material, from which a materialistic philosophy starts is incapable of evolution. This material is in itself the ultimate substance. Evolution, on the (mechanical) materialistic theory, is reduced to the role of being another word for the description of the changes of the external relations between portions of matter. There is nothing to evolve, because one set of external relations is as good as any other set of external relations. There can merely be change, purposeless and unprogressive. But the whole point of the modern doctrine is the evolution of the complex organisms from the antecedent states of less complex organisms. The doctrine thus cries aloud for a conception of organism as fundamental for nature. It also requires an underlying activity—a substantial activity—expressing itself in individual embodiments, and evolving in achievements of organisms.[7]

The underlying activity—the substantial activity—that Whitehead speaks of here seems to correspond to the "spiritual power" of nature in Teilhard's doctrine. It is God Himself immanent to the universe—God Himself working along with His creation through His creative power. This power or activity is indicative of God for Whitehead as well as for Teilhard. But Whitehead's only God is this immanent one. Quite the contrary for Teilhard. For him, it is the Transcendent, Infinite God Who is Within the universe, though infinitely superior to it. His creative power, which as coming from Him is spiritual or psychic in nature, is the source of all the tangential and radial forms of energy in the world. Yet neither God nor His creative power at work in the world, are to be confused with the things in the world, which are the *effects* of that power.

Thus, Teilhard is not a pantheist. Henri de Lubac has shown this very clearly in his book—a defense of the man and his philosophy—*Teilhard de Chardin: The Man and His Meaning*. Even Aldous Huxley in the Introduction to *The Phenomenon of Man* points this out in these unambiguous words:

> Belief in the pre-eminence of personality was for Teilhard a matter of faith supported by rational inquiry and scientific knowledge, which prevented

---

[7] *Science and the Modern World* (p. 151), as quoted in Schilipp, *op. cit.*, pp. 257-258.

Teilhard and Modern Thought

Teilhard's concept of the immanence of God in the world from becoming a vague and meaningless pantheism. (PM, 19-20)

God is the center of evolution, a personal provident God, "directing the universe with loving, watchful care." Teilhard explains:

> As early as in St. Paul and St. John we read that to create, to fulfil and to purify the world is, for God, to unify it by uniting it organically with Himself. How does He unify it? By partially immersing Himself in things, by becoming "element", and then, from this point of vantage in the heart of matter, assuming the control and leadership of what we now call evolution. (PM, 293-294)

God for Whitehead is immanent in the world, yet seemingly lacks all transcendent character. Hence, while both Whitehead and Teilhard believe in a God immanent in evolving nature, only Teilhard's God is both immanent and transcendent. Through His creative power God has immersed Himself into His creation without losing His transcendence. Scientifically, to both Whitehead and Teilhard God is immanent to the world through His active power in the universe. But according to Teilhard, this same God is, in Himself, infinite and transcendent—a truth which can be known both by rational philosophy and Christian Faith. Whitehead, on the other hand, will not go beyond the creative power of God in the universe and thus recognizes only an immanent God. Despite his failure to go further, however, Whitehead must be credited for his recognition of divine immanence and finality in evolution, which is denied by Darwin and others.

Darwin's *On the Origin of the Species* has had a great impact on science and philosophy. Not least among the results of his influence is the idea of "struggle for existence" and "adaptation to environment" or, together, "survival of the fittest." Inherent in Darwin's theory is the purposelessness or aimlessness of evolution, an evolution that has no meaningful finality. Whitehead was severely critical of these aspects of Darwinian evolutionism. He had, as Johnson says, "scant respect" for them.[8] This aimlessness was also alien to Teilhard's philosophy and science. To Darwin evolution was only a transformation of zoological species; to Teilhard it was an "unalterable interconnection of all existence in the cosmos from the first atom up to mankind."[9]

In *The Function of Reason* Whitehead refutes the Darwinian concept of a purposeless evolution. Whitehead did not mollify his words:

> The fallacy is the belief that fitness for survival is identical with the best exemplification of the Art of Life....In fact life itself is comparatively deficient in survival value. The art of persistence is to be dead. Only inorganic things persist for great lengths of time. A rock survives for eight million years; whereas the limit for a tree is about a thousand years....They certainly did not appear because they were better at that game than the rocks around them.[10]

Whitehead continues his blast: He says that the world is

---

[8] A. H. Johnson, *Whitehead's Theory of Reality*. (New York: Dover Publications, 1962), p. 165.
[9] J. V. Kopp, *Teilhard de Chardin*. (New York: Paulist Press, 1965), p. 46.
[10] Whitehead, *The Function of Reason, op. cit.*, p. 4.

Teilhard and Modern Thought

suffering from a bad attack of "muddle-headed" positivism which advocates that nature has no aim but is just purposeless. Is there then no connection between the bee and the flower, he asks. The world is suffering from the disease of Descartes' dualism. As already pointed out, he writes:

> The effect of this sharp division between nature and life has poisoned all subsequent philosophy.... Neither physical nature nor life can be understood unless we fuse them together as essential factors in the composition of "really real" things whose interconnections and individual characters constitute the universe.[11]

Whitehead used to point to the trend upward in evolution, the conduct of human affairs, and man's active attack on his environment for added proof against the purposelessness of Darwin's evolution.

Teilhard in *The Future of Man* doesn't mention Darwin explicitly, yet he refutes Darwin much like Whitehead—with science:

> While accepting the undeniable fact of the general evolution of Life in the course of time, many biologists still maintain that those changes take place without any defined course, in any direction and at random. The contention, disastrous to the idea of progress, is refuted, in my view, by the tremendous fact of the continuing of "cerebralization" of living creatures. (FM, 65)

Teilhard and Whitehead use, more or less, the same

---

11 Schilipp, *op. cit.*, pp. 266-267.

scientific proofs to refute Darwin. Yet, the specific finality or end, that towards which the evolutionary process is tending, is radically different. For Whitehead the end of evolution is increased complexity of organisms. "The organism," Whitehead states, "is a unit of emergent value, a real fusion of the character of eternal objects, emerging *for its own sake.*" (Schilpp, p. 233) If this is Whitehead's sole reason for evolution, it is hard to see why Whitehead believes in an immanent God, as Bochenski points out in his *Contemporary European Philosophy* (pp. 233-235).

Teilhard, on the other hand, believes that the end and direction of evolution is the Omega point which is already in existence and operative at the very core of the thinking mass. The end of the world Teilhard calls a "wholesale internal introversion upon itself of the noosphere..., the overthrow of equilibrium...rest(ing) with all its weight on God-Omega." (PM, 287-288) The finality of Teilhard is, then, simply union with God.

Teilhard, like Whitehead, was very aware of evolution as indicative of a divine immanence in nature. But Teilhard, as a Christian, saw this recognition as common ground from which he hoped to bring scientists to a Christian viewpoint. On the other hand, he was intent on convincing Christians of an awareness of God's presence in nature (a "natural" presence, recognizable by a scientist), which the Christian might tend to overlook. In this double objective, Teilhard was not successful during his lifetime. After his death, however, his writings are making better headway. Nevertheless, to achieve the objective, the method of Teilhard de Chardin must be understood. This will be the subject of the next essay.

8.

THE METHOD OF TEILHARD

To some, the world has disclosed itself as too vast: within such immensity, man is lost and no longer counts; and there is nothing left to him to do but shut his eyes and disappear. To others, on the contrary, the world is too beautiful; and it, and it alone, must be adored. (DM, 45)

In previous essays we have seen that Teilhard's thought bears resemblances to the Thomistic school, to the Franciscan school, and to modern schools of thought. How is such a combination possible? We submit that it springs from a method which has its roots in the well-known formula, *Fides Quaerens Intellectum* (Faith seeking understanding) of St. Anselm, who lived almost a thousand years ago and who is known as the "Father of Scholastic Philosophy."

In St. Anselm's wisdom, faith stands as the indispensable starting point.[1] It is from the word of God that we must learn the truth which subsequently we must strive to understand. In a living faith the warmth of love is never absent from the light of understanding. That "faith to

---

[1] See Gerald B. Phelan, *The Wisdom of St. Anselm*. (Latrobe, Pa.: Archabbey Press, 1960).

understand" is a vital faith—something which is the answer to all our yearnings, in which the whole purpose of life and being is fulfilled, a faith operative and motivating one's whole life and outlook on life.

By faith Teilhard knew that Christ is the Alpha and Omega, the very center of the universe, in whom all things hold together. On the other hand, from his knowledge of science and of the attitude of scientists of modern times, he accepted a world in evolution—a universe moving forward. The question he asked himself was the mystery posed by the contemporary world in which he lives. Teilhard saw that:

> ...what makes the world in which we live specifically modern is our discovery in it and around it of evolution. And I can now add that what disconcerts the modern world at its very roots is not being sure, and not seeing how it ever could be sure, that there is an outcome—a *suitable outcome*—to that evolution. (PM, 229)

The very complexity and immensity of the universe compel man to search for a philosophy interpreting this fact. Our search today is the same as for all time—what is the meaning of the world, why am I here, and who is God? But the terrifying picture of today is that these questions are scientific as well as philosophic—at least in the sense that they naturally arise in the mind of the scientist against the background of a world in evolution. It was the great hope of Teilhard, as a scientist and Christian philosopher to find a satisfactory answer to these great questions. He held that the meaning of man and the evolution of the world could not be separated. And, by an analysis of the system whereby the universe increases and progresses, Teilhard conceived the goal of the universe precisely as that of achieving consciousness of its purpose in and through man. The world, as we find it today, culminates in man—the conscious being; and Teilhard reasons that this requires for its cause a Person—creating and directing the world towards a conscious goal: the super-consciousness of all persons in that One Person.

Cosmogenesis was the first phase of evolution. Matter was formed from energy and assumed ever more complex forms as time passed. The second phase or critical point of evolution was biogenesis. This is the evolutionary process by which living organisms change from one species to another over extended periods of time. The next critical point was the greatest of all. Out of the quiet labyrinth of time came a self-reflecting being. All evolution had tended toward that great step. The whole purpose and direction of evolution culminated in man. The next critical point, according to Teilhard, will be the convergence on the Point Omega. As he says in *The Phenomenon of Man:*

> All our difficulties and repulsions as regards the opposition between the All and the Person would be dissipated if only we understood that, by structure, the noosphere (and more generally the world) represent a whole that is not only closed but also centered. Because it contains and engenders consciousness, space-time is necessarily of a convergent nature. Accordingly, its enormous layers, followed in the right direction, must somewhere ahead become involuted to a point which we might call Omega, which fuses and consumes them integrally in itself. (PM, 259)

Thus the world, created for God, will actually culminate in God in the Person of Christ, Who is Point Omega.

His Inspiration

All Teilhard's writings were strongly motivated by the Jesuit motto: Ad Majorem Dei Gloriam. As he himself stated in the preface to his *Divine Milieu:*

> My hope is that it (*The Divine Milieu*) may help to show that Christ, who is ever the same and ever new, has not ceased to be the "first" within mankind. (DM, 43)

Teilhard was first of all a priest and a Jesuit, then a scientist, philosopher, theologian, author and poet. He tried to reconcile the demands of scientific philosophy with what Christian hope postulates, especially as regards the end of the world and of man, for this is the extremely important topic for him.

What was going to happen to man was very clearly evident to Teilhard:

> Underlying all the surface-changes of present-day history, the reality and permanent importance of a single basic event is becoming daily more manifest: namely, the rise of the masses, with its natural corollary, the socialization of mankind. (FM, 124)

Teilhard so firmly believed the fact that man was destined for a glorious future, and that signs were pointing to this already, that he repeated the thought over and over:

> In spite of all evidence to the contrary, mankind may be very well advancing all around us at the moment—there are in fact many signs whereby we can reasonably suppose that it is advancing. (PM, 255)

> The world is a-building. This is the basic truth which first must be understood so thoroughly that it becomes an habitual and as it were natural springboard for our thinking.
> Laboriously, though, and thanks to the activity of mankind, the new earth is being formed and purified and is taking on definition and clarity. (HU, 92-93)

> [The Mongolian journey] has confirmed me in my faith in the future. The world holds no interest for me unless I look forward but when my eyes are on the future it is full of excitement. (LT, 104)

And the glorious future that he envisioned was definitely the unity of all mankind:

> The general gathering together in which, by correlated actions of the *"without"* and the *"within"* of the earth, the totality of thinking units and thinking forces are engaged—the aggregation in a single block of all mankind, whose fragments weld together and interpenetrate before our eyes in spite of (indeed in proportion to) their efforts to separate. (PM, 243)

> But more specifically still, he [man] represents the only case in the field of our experience of a species which (because at once reflective by nature and planetary in extension—the one because of the other) tends irresistibly to knit itself together materially and psychologically until it forms in the strict biological sense, a single super-organism of a definite nature. (VP, 265)

Pages of quotations would lend little more than weight, but pages could be added. Teilhard envisioned a tremendous unity for mankind. The thought was so definite in his mind that it came out in his scientific works, his mystical works, and even in his personal letters.

The reasons Pere Teilhard presented to support his idea of collectivization were many. First of all, on the natural level, the pressing together of men caused by their increasing numbers and relationships would force them closer together by the growth of common power, common interests, and common needs. (FM, 306) But just as a certain energy was necessary for the earlier evolutionary leap from unconsciousness to conscious thought, for an association of consciousnesses there is also a need of dynamic energy which would cause the desired unity. That dynamic energy is love. As Rideau put it:

> And, if we must recognize that the energy that builds the universe, and still more the universe of man, is an energy of love, then there is only one name that can be rightly given to God, the name of love. It is, then, only through him and in him that man and the universe attain their end.[2]

Just becoming aware of this fact was important for Teilhard, it would enable collectivization to pass from the enforced stage into a free phase where men will not only understand their real place as inseparably joined elements of a converging whole, but also a natural union of affinity and sympathy would supersede compulsion. (FM, 125) This is a major step on the actual road to unity.

In all this, however, the most essential element is missing, as can be surmised from the words of Emile Rideau just quoted. It is undeniably true that Teilhard believed

---

2 Emile Rideau, *The Thought of Teilhard de Chardin,* trans. by Rene Hague. (New York: Harper & Row, 1967), p. 60.

that man was tending toward unity, but the natural union of man was not his final end. The actual destiny of men and of all creation and evolution is communion in and through something (actually Someone) that Teilhard called the Omega Point. According to the eminent Jesuit's thought, mankind must accept the existence of a higher center of consciousness at the apogee of evolution. If one reflects on this fact it will become quite clear to him that a mere unity of mankind perfected by human love will not be sufficient. Whatever possesses the capability of joining together the whole world must be above all that is in the world, it must be ultra-conscious, ultra-personalized, ultra-present. (FM, 92) This finality is what Teilhard termed the Omega Point; not a point but a Person—Jesus Christ:

> God the Centre of centres. In that final vision the Christian dogma culminates. And so exactly, so perfectly does this coincide with the Omega Point that doubtless I should never have ventured to envisage the latter or formulate the hypothesis rationally if, in my consciousness as a believer, I had not found only its speculative model but also its living reality. (PM, 294)

Teilhard repeated this fact frequently: to reach Omega evolution was futile and meaningless unless Omega were perceived as a living person.

> I discovered that everything was again centered upon a Point, upon a Person, and this Person was you, Jesus![3]

---

[3] Pierre Teilhard de Chardin, *Escrits du Temps de la Guerre, 1916-1919* (Paris, 1965), as quoted in Christopher F. Mooney, *Teilhard de Chardin and the Mystery of Christ*. (New York: Garden City, 1964), p. 27.

Or as he wrote elsewhere:

> Hence the importance, or rather the necessity, of a Christology in which there is a correspondence between the human point of planetary maturation and the Christic point of the Parousia.[4]

The role of the Personal Christ cannot, however, be viewed simply as an end. First of all, no creature could uplift himself to reach the level of unity with God unless God wished that there be a union. That is to say: "Nothing can come to Christ unless he himself takes it and gathers it to himself." (HU, 152) Or better still:

> By its very structure, the noosphere could not close itself either individually or socially in any way save under the influence of the centre we have called Omega. (PM, 291)

Secondly, the action of the Parousia is not inevitable. Man has control of the forces of evolution, so he must use them to bring about that human unity, the unity of consciousness, which is the prerequisite of final unity totally with Christ.[5]

The accomplishment of this entails a purgation; man must turn away from his own selfish interest to God:

> But because the term toward which the earth is moving lies not merely beyond each individual thing but beyond the totality of things; because the world travails, not to bring forth from within itself some

---

[4] Pierre Teilhard de Chardin, *Comment Je Vois* (1948), as quoted in Mooney, *ibid.,* pp. 68-69.
[5] Rideau, *op. cit.,* p. 181.

The Method of Teilhard

supreme reality, but to find its consummation through a union with a pre-existent Being; it follows that man can never reach the blazing centre of the universe simply by living more and more for himself nor even by spending his life in the service of some earthly cause however great. The world can never be definitively united with you, Lord, save by a sort of reversal, a turning about, an *excentration,* which must involve the temporary collapse not merely of all individual achievements but even of anything that looks like an advancement for humanity. (HU, 31)

In brief then, the entire evolutionary cycle is thrust on by the power of Christ the Omega in cooperation with the activity of man. This is because:

...the cosmic function of Omega consists in initiating and maintaining within its radius the unanimity of the world's "reflective" particles....Neither an ideal centre, nor a potential centre could possibly suffice. A present and real noosphere goes with a real and present centre. To be supremely attractive, Omega must be supremely present. (PM, 269)

The way in which Omega became supremely present in the evolutionary process was through the life, death and Resurrection of Jesus of Nazareth. In the real Person of Jesus the real Omega became part of the evolutionary current for which he himself is responsible. Christ's whole work of salvation thus became rooted in space-time and was destined to continue until fulfillment.[6] The power to continue on the evolutionary path to Omega, to repeat

---

6 Mooney, *op. cit.,* pp. 69-70.

again, comes from Christ, but it comes through the instrument of his Church, through Christianity.

> Christianity is not, as it is sometimes presented and sometimes practised, an additional burden of observances and obligations to weigh down and increase the already heavy load or to multiply the already paralysing ties of our life in society. It is, if fact, a soul of immense power which bestows immense significance and beauty and a new lightness on what we are already doing. (DM, 70)

Or, as Teilhard wrote later in his life:

> At the very heart of the social phenomenon, a kind of *ultra-socialization* is in progress: that whereby the "Church" is being formed little by little, vivifying by its influence and collecting under their sublimest form all the spiritual energies of the noosphere; the Church, reflectively "Christified" portion of the world; the Church, main focus of inter-human affinities via super-charity; the Church, central axis of universal convergence and the exact point of encounter flashing between universe and the Omega Point.[7]

The union of all men, as envisioned by Teilhard, stands in stark contrast to the union of mankind as proposed by Marxism. But the point must be made that both foresee the same outcome of evolution—human solidarity and union, to which the world is tending.

So far Teilhard shares this view with behaviourist psychology and with the social sciences of man which

---

[7] *Comment Je Vois,* 24, as quoted in Henri de Lubac, *Teilhard Explained,* trans. by Anthony Buono. (Glen Rock, N.J.: Paulist Press, 1968), p. 25.

are based upon biology, instinct, cultural and economic conditions, and which (like Marxism) are usually opposed to the religious views of man. For Teilhard, however, it is only part of the picture, even if it is an indispensable part. Anterior and exterior causal factors...cannot fully explain man's character.[8]

Teilhard agreed with what scientists expressed concerning man, (excluding religion up to a point) just as Marx did, but he could not stop there. The spiritual nature of man and the spiritual power which, in Christian belief, directs the course of the historic development, would not allow him to end up only with man.

Following this point directly is the fact that Teilhard saw religion in a much different way than did Marx and his followers. He wrote:

> Religion has sometimes been understood as a mere antidote to our evils, an "opiate". Its true purpose is to sustain and spur on the progress of life. It is the profound need of an Absolute, sought from the start through every progressive form of religion....Religion is not an option or a strictly individual intuition, but represents the long unfolding, the collective experience of all mankind, of the existence of God-God reflecting himself personally on the organized sum of thinking beings to guarantee a sure result of creation, and to lay down exact laws for man's hesitant activities. (BE, 59-60, 63)

There is no other way to express it; Teilhard could not see evolution and man without religion and God.

---

[8] Michael H. Murray, *The Thought of Teilhard de Chardin.* (New York: Seabury Press, 1966), p. 41.

So, what then can be said about the relationship of Marxism and "Teilhardian" Christianity? For instance, what did Teilhard think of Marxism? Since Teilhard lived after Marx and was able to observe the results of Marxist philosophy as it was put into practice by Lenin and Stalin in Russia, he did make some comments on it. He did not like Marxism basically because it envisioned an end which necessarily excluded God. Furthermore, due to the rejection of God, he felt that Marxists could never reach what they claimed was their goal.

> All their worship of material progress and race as an entity to be preserved will never produce freedom: they are inevitably absorbed and assimilated by the forces of determinism they build up. They become mechanized by their own mechanical institutions. And the only way now left for them to control the working elements of human energy is to use brute force—the force that—logically enough, they are now beginning again to try and make us worship.[9]

Communism not only destroys its purpose, human freedom, but excludes any chance for a spiritually uplifting end for the universe:

> ...in its unbalanced admiration of the physical powers of the universe, it [Communism] has systematically excluded from its hopes the possibility of a spiritual metamorphosis of the universe. (BE, 28)

Thus it becomes quite clear that a close relationship

---

[9] Pierre Teilhard de Chardin, *Savons l'humanite* (1937), in *Cahiers Pierre Teilhard de Chardin,* No 1, p. 26, as quoted in Rideau, *op. cit.,* p. 479.

between Teilhard and Karl Marx cannot be envisioned. Their systems do not allow a close relationship for they obviously disagree on a very fundamental premise: the existence and role of God. But it cannot be denied that the unity of man which Marx posited, taken simply as a fact, is also a fact posited by Teilhard. Moreover, Marx's emphasis on the necessity of working for this world to create the unity of man is of extreme value for Teilhard. But again there is the fundamental disagreement as to end.

All that can be said in conclusion is that men cannot really be forced to believe something. True belief demands the assent of the will. Men have followed the system of Karl Marx because they thought it presented answers to the questions that most disturbed them. If they are satisfied with these answers and are convinced that they are correct, then there is not much a Christian can do except explain the position of Christianity, especially as it is envisioned by Teilhard de Chardin, pray that the gift of Faith be given, and show by the example of life that Christianity exceeds Marx in understanding man and in offering him true peace and eternal happiness.

Conclusion

Returning, then, to the question of method in Teilhard de Chardin, we can only say that, if we are to judge it by its fruits, only time will tell whether it proves to be a successful antidote to Marxism.

But if we judge it a priori, then we can compare it either with the methodology of St. Anselm, or with the more rigid procedure of St. Thomas Aquinas. In either case, some favorable points can be made.

First of all, we suggest that Teilhard's method is a twentieth century application of the *Fides quaerens intellectum* (Faith seeking understanding), popularized by St. Anselm. Knowing by faith that Christ, the God-Man, is the center of the universe, Teilhard seeks to find a reason how this is so. His knowledge of modern science, and specifically his awareness of creative energy at the heart of the evolutionary process, prompts him to envision the Incarnate Word of God, risen from the dead as the controller of the world's creative energy. He thus can come to the knowledge, through faith, of the purpose of the evolutionary process so controlled: the consummation of all things in God through the eventual consciousness of man of the evolutionary process itself.

However, Teilhard's confidence in his conclusions are subject to the same criticism sometimes directed against St. Anselm. In the *Cur Deus Homo,* the Saint lays down the principle: where anything is proposed as unfitting to God as by faith we know Him to be, we must conclude that it is impossible; on the other hand, whenever we see even the slightest reason, provided that there is nothing else contrary to it, we may conclude to its necessity. This is the principle which he uses to show that anything which is contrary to the truth as we know it (whether it concerns God or the things which He has said or made) is unreasonable and false.[10] This principle is sometimes called the Franciscan principle of optimism. In St. Anselm's case, it resulted in the Saint's speaking of the Incarnation as apparently necessary. Similarly, in Teilhard, it causes him to speak as if the natural order postulates and evolves into the supernatural necessarily. His utterances seem to suggest

---

10 See Phelan, *op. cit.*

The Method of Teilhard 109

that no other creation than an evolutionary one is possible. So developed, the principle completely overstates the case; as St. Anselm himself is sometimes accused in his own use of the principle.

If Teilhard's approach is similar to St. Anselm's and subject to the same misapplication, how does it compare with the method of St. Thomas Aquinas? In philosophical matters, Thomas proceeds from the evidence of outside reality, known through the senses, to rational deductions in various areas. Thus, he proves the existence of God from the order in the cosmos. Basically, Teilhard proceeds in the same way. The difference lies in the *greater evidence* available to Teilhard. Evident to Teilhard, as to his fellow scientists, is a world in evolution. The conclusion reached by not a few scientist philosophers known to Teilhard, was that there is a cosmic energy at work in the world. This cosmic energy was variously interpreted by different thinkers. Teilhard insists that the cosmic energy is nothing else than the creative power of God immanent in the world. However, he also teaches that the God immanent in the universe is Infinite in Himself and hence transcendent in the traditional sense. "In Him," he says, "everything rises up as towards a focus-point of immanence, but from Him, too, everything comes down as though from a peak of transcendence."[11] Thus he takes a truth partly recognized by his contemporaries and re-interprets it in the light of sound reason, which never contradicts Faith.

However, we must admit that in his expressions and in his manner of presentation, Teilhard sometimes allows himself to depart from the strict rigor characteristic of the

---

[11] Quoted by Henri de Lubac, *The Religion of Teilhard de Chardin.* (New York: Desclee, 1967), p. 181.

intellectualistic method of St. Thomas. Nevertheless, in so doing, he seems to be using a channel of knowledge which is also recognized by St. Thomas as basically valid, viz., knowledge by connaturality. By a sort of intuitive knowledge, Teilhard not only understands but "feels" the cosmic presence of God and the divine creative power which fills the universe. Since other scientist philosophers seem to have had a similar sense (though differently interpreted) should not Teilhard be given the liberty to express this important discovery and to incorporate it into the "philosophia perennis?"

In a letter written in 1919, Teilhard wrote that his concern was to discover the conditions for progress as open for modern man, and not to start from first principles in a theoretical development of the universe. He foresaw that this method would alienate him to professional philosophers, but he felt that his strength rested in being faithful to the vision granted him. "Others," he wrote, "can bring me into line with the principles, if they can." (*ibid.,* 86)

Meanwhile, he continued to enjoy a mystic experience of the truth that after his death would be widely shared through his writings; and in proportion to the success that his writings have in communicating his genuine message, his method must be judged valid.

> "Sometimes," he wrote in 1926, "when I am immersed in rocks and fossils, I experience a nameless bliss in remembering that I possess, in one total, incorruptible and loving Element, the Supreme Principle in which all subsists and has life. 'Per quem omnia semper bona creas, vivificas, sanctificas et praestas nobis,' we say at Mass. What science and

The Method of Teilhard

what philosophy could compare with the knowledge of that Reality—and above all with its perception, however modest and embryonic it may be." (*ibid.*, 89)

Will modern scientists, and before them, Christians themselves come to realize, not only that their own personal fulfillment is in Christ, but that the whole evolution of the universe must find its fulfillment in Him?

We suggest that the answer to this question is also the answer to the question of the validity of Teilhard's method. In summary, let us say that, *as a believer,* Teilhard has a right to follow in the tradition of "faith seeking understanding" and to seek in evolution the answer to the question how the world is centered in Christ. Then, it is only natural that he present to his fellow-believers his own convictions in confirmation of their faith. On the other hand, *as a scientist philosopher,* he has the right, even the duty, to suggest a rational culmination of the evolutionary spiral in a First Mover and Final Cause. And he has an advantage over Aristotle and previous philosophers because, with good reason, he can point out to his fellow scientists that the First Mover and Final Cause has appeared in human history in the Person of Jesus Christ. Science, Reason, Faith, and Apologetics thus converge in one vision of hope. In a word, Teilhard says to his fellow scientists: you need an explanation for evolution which is reasonable and verifiable. Consider the one that I am proposing. And to his fellow believers, Teilhard says: Have faith in Christ, not only for your own personal salvation and for the Church, but in His power over the whole universe, over which He has personal control, and in His Will to save the whole human race. Totally cooperate in His plan of total salvation for the human species, which He has brought to maturity, notwithstanding all the forces of the antichrist and of hell itself. This is the victory that has overcome the world: our faith!

9.

OVERLOOKED ASPECTS OF TEILHARD'S THOUGHT

These essays have designedly been called "aspects" of Teilhard's thought. The reason for this is that our purpose has not been to present a synthesis of Teilhard's worldview such as might be gathered from his own writings. Many works on Teilhard—and, indeed, Teilhard's own numerous writings—serve this purpose. Our intention has been to bring together from various schools of philosophy certain key concepts which are re-echoed by Teilhard in tones perhaps more in tune with contemporary man. Thus, Aristotle's "Unmoved Mover," if conceived as an efficient, as well as a final cause, finds an echo in Teilhard's Alpha and Omega Point of Evolution. The all-encompassing function of *act* and *potency* of St. Thomas finds a counterpart in the twofold energy of Teilhard—radial energy (which in its basic manifestation is the very creative power of God Himself) and tangential energy (with its inherent capacity for physical measurement). The *light* of St. Bonaventure finds its reflection in Teilhard's *luminous energy,* which is the most basic manifestation of matter itself. The *elan vital* of Bergson, as well as the "mysterious impulse" of Whitehead, corresponds to the "spiritual power" in Teilhard, who divines the presence and action of the Creative Spirit in the evolution of the world.

114 *Aspects of the Thought of Teilhard de Chardin*

Now it remains to point out two very important elements in Teilhard's thought which, if overlooked, could lead to unacceptable misinterpretations of his thought. Both these elements center around the generally recognized *optimism* of Teilhard. If his optimism is viewed in isolation from the necessity of *man's action* or from God's *directive influence,* a number of erroneous positions could result and, in fact, have resulted.

The Hour of Choice

In the *Future of Man,* Teilhard states the case very clearly and somewhat at length:

> In every sphere, physical no less than intellectual and moral, and whether it be a question of flowing water, a traveller on a journey, or a thinker or mystic engaged in the pursuit of truth, there inevitably comes a point in time and place when the necessity presents itself, to mechanical forces, or to our freedom of choice, of deciding once and for all which of two paths is the one to take. The enforced, irrevocable choice at a parting of the ways that will never occur again: which of us has not encountered that dilemma? But how many of us realise that it is precisely the situation in which social man finds himself, *here and now,* in the face of the rising tide of socialisation?
>
> Borne on a current of Totalisation that is taking shape and gathering speed around us, we cannot, as I have said, either stop or turn back. Indeed, how can we even contemplate escaping from a tide that is not only planetary but cosmic in its dimensions?
>
> As I have also shown, two attitudes are possible in this situation, two forms of "existentialism." We can

reject and resist the tide, seeking by every means to slow it down and even to escape individually (at the risk of perishing in stoical isolation) from what looks like a rush to the abyss; or we can yield to it and actively contribute to what we accept as a liberating and life-giving movement.

It remains for us to demonstrate the urgency of the problem; that is to say, to fulfil my purpose by showing that we have truly reached the parting of the ways, the point where the waters divide; and also to show that in this momentous hour we cannot continue physically to exist (to act) without deciding here and now which of the two attitudes we shall adopt: that of defiance or that of faith in the unification of mankind. (FM, 254-255)

Teilhard treats of the same problem at the conclusion of *The Phenomenon of Man.* There, he explains that the unification of mankind is not the *ultimate* of human destiny. The final destiny is *union with God,* which, "according to a first hypothesis" more acceptable to him, he envisions as taking place *in peace,* even though with some unavoidable tension.

But, he continues, there is another possibility. Obeying a law, from which nothing in the past has ever been exempt, evil may go on growing alongside good, and it too may attain its paroxysm at the end in some specifically new form.

There are no summits without abysses.

Enormous powers will be liberated in mankind by the inner play of its cohesion: though it may be that this energy will still be displayed discordantly tomor-

> row, as today and in the past. Are we to foresee a mechanising synergy under brute force or a synergy of sympathy? Are we to foresee man seeking to fulfil himself collectively upon himself, or personally on a greater than himself? Refusal or acceptance of Omega? A conflict may supervene. In that case the noosphere, in the course of and by virtue of the process which draws it together, will, when it has reached its point of unification, split into two zones each attracted to an opposite pole of adoration. Thought has never completely united upon itself here below. Universal love would only vivify and detach finally a fraction of the noosphere so as to consummate it—the part which decided to "cross the threshhold", to get outside itself into the other. *Ramification once again, for the last time.* (PM, 288-289)

Teilhard's "hour of choice," then, does not exclude, but rather implies that ultimate progress is incompatible with a global and voluntary rejection of God. This, in turn, implies on a global scale the voluntary rejection of evil, which obviously has been present in history, to the detriment of the over-all progress of the world. We are reminded of St. Augustine's conflict of the two cities. The point is that free men must work towards the goal of human unity and God's glory, overcoming opposing forces, yet knowing that there is no natural assurance of the immediate outcome of this effort. Nor is there question of indefinite progress. Quite the contrary.

> Not an indefinite progress, which is an hypothesis contradicted by the convergent nature of noogenesis, but an ecstasy transcending the dimensions and the framework of the visible universe.

Overlooked Aspects of Teilhard's Thought 117

Ecstasy in concord; or discord; but in either case by excess of interior tension: the only biological outcome proper to or conceivable for the phenomenon of man. (PM, 289)

The Idea of Time

The rejection of the idea of indefinite progress is in line with Teilhard's conception of time. In *The Future of Man*, he writes:

...why not define Time itself as precisely the rise of the Universe into those high latitudes whose complexity, centration, concentration, and consciousness grow and increase simultaneously and correlatively? (FM, 88)

Teilhard's is a time which measures evolutionary development, from which it takes its meaning. Time had its beginning, just as evolution had its beginning; and it will have its end in Christogenesis, the peak of hominization and point of critical reflection, the fulfillment of all evolution. Time itself can be measured by the advance of evolution, and the speed of time by the speed of evolution. Time cannot go back, as evolution is irreversible, but it can appear to man to go slower or faster, according to the lesser or greater number of events happening in its passage. In this sense, we can refer to Teilhard's concept of time as evolutionary time, although Teilhard himself prefers the terms, "organic" time, "biological" time, or "space-time."

In the words of Rideau:

In addition to the space that mesmerized Pascal, we now have time: not a time that is simply in a container in which years are stored side by side, but an organic time, measured by the development of global reality. Formerly, we used to look on ourselves and the things around us as self-contained points. Now we see that beings are like insubstantial fibers woven into a universal process. Everything sinks back into the boundless depths of the past, and everything is flung into the boundless depths of the future. In its history, every being is coextensive with the whole of duration.[1]

In Thomistic terminology we can put it this way: every individual being is related by multiple relationships, so that in its total reality it has connections back to the origin of the universe. In a figure of speech, Teilhard compares things to a garment—the garment of evolution—in which each thing is similar to a thread woven in the whole. Teilhard also suggests a simile for evolutionary time:

> We still hesitate, as I have said, over the form which we may conveniently attribute to space-time....Caught within its curve the layers of matter (considered as separate elements no less than as a whole) tighten and converge in thought, by synthesis. Therefore, it is as a cone, in the form of a cone, that it can be depicted. (FM, 88)

In this cone, then, evolutionary time is the constant progress forward of evolution, and space is the momentary section of the flow of time. (FM, 84)

Evolutionary time, then, serves as a measure of the progress of evolution, as far as this is possible at any given point of history. Evolutionary time gives us a better understanding of the dimensions and importance of every element of evolution.

---

[1] Rideau, *The Thought of Teilhard de Chardin, op. cit.,* p. 303.

Overlooked Aspects of Teilhard's Thought

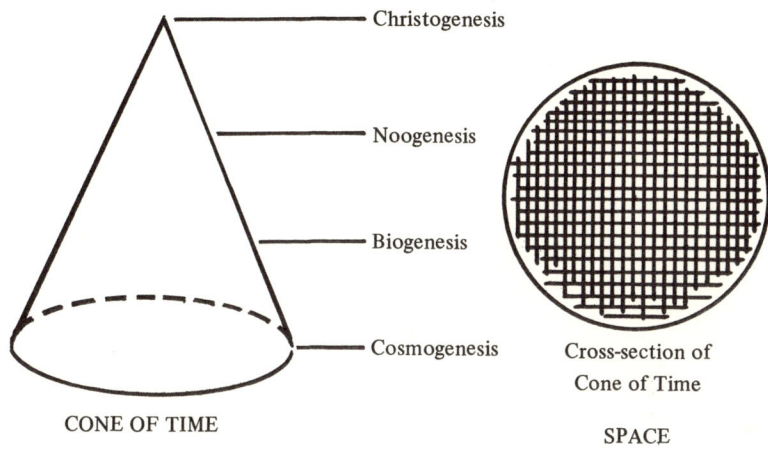

The perception of organic time of which we are speaking (that is of time whose total unrolling corresponds to the gradual and progressive and irreversible elaboration of a collection of organically linked elements), this new perception, we say does not offer in itself any explanation of things, but only a more correct view of their quantitative integrity. By the fact that living beings, for example, instead of being confined within a few years existence, now appear to us as the fruit of a gestation which makes them literally children of the earth and universe, we come to appreciate more exactly their dimensions and the immensity of the problem posed by the material existence of the smallest of them. (VP, 130-131)

Evolutionary time cannot reverse direction (this is because evolution itself is irreversible). However, evolutionary time can appear to speed up or accelerate. This is easily seen by two phenomena: (a) the actual speeding up of evolution; and (b) the great technological advancement in the recent era.

All of Teilhard's models and diagrams of evolution constantly show us a quickening of the pace of evolution, as man nears the goal. Man is closer now than he ever was to the conclusion of his pilgrimage on earth. He is running, indeed, sprinting towards the finish line. Teilhard himself declares:

> Far from appearing to be slowing up or reaching its ceiling around us, this biological movement of pan-human convergence has simply been entering a comprehensive phase in which it is bound to accelerate from now on. (AM, 245)

The great technological achievements of today point to the acceleration of evolution and therefore the acceleration of evolutionary time.

Ernst Benz explains:

> ...the technology of antiquity lacked the twofold element which became decisive for the unexpected growth of technology in the Christian West: the element of progress, and the element of acceleration.... It occurs in a dramatic acceleration directed toward a certain goal, brought about because the struggle between the forces of the old age and the new age leads to ever more violent blows and counter-blows and because this struggle presses itself toward a final decision.[2]

---

[2] Ernst Benz, *Evolution and Christian Hope*. (New York: Garden City, 1966), pp. 126-127.

As Teilhard sees it, now that man has partially realized himself in evolution, soon he will globally realize this forward pushing process and at this point he will be called to use his technology to stride the last steps to Christogenesis at unimaginable speeds. Meanwhile, as technology itself accelerates, each advance is important. Teilhard gives an example:

> ...I am also thinking of the insidious growth of those astonishing electronic computers which, pulsating with signals at the rate of hundreds of thousands a second, not only relieve our brains of tedious and exhausting work, but because they enhance the essential (and too little noted) factor of "speed of thought," are also paving the way for a revolution in the sphere of research. (FM, 167)

Though the influence of technology has been predominant especially in the Western Countries, the impact of their development has been world wide. Even if sometimes for the wrong reasons, technology is contributing to the unification of mankind. Earlier in the century Teilhard could point out that within the half century technology made incredible progress: not technics of a dispersed and local kind but a closely interdependent network of enterprises over the whole earth.

Christogenesis and God's Directive Influence

In Teilhard's perspective, when will Christogenesis occur? In the first place, he says:

> ...despite an almost explosive acceleration of noogenesis at our level, we cannot expect to see the earth transform itself under our eyes in the space of a generation. (PM, 255)

Taking a longer view, in *The Future of Man,* he ventured the following prediction:

> Structurally and notwithstanding any impression or appearance to the contrary, man is at present engaged in a process within which (by the very use of his liberty—that is to say in order to survive and transcend) he is compelled (at least statistically) to an ever increasing biological self-unification. Therefore, right in front of us in time, a peak of hominisation must necessarily exist—a peak which, to judge by the enormous quantity of unarranged humanity still all around us, must certainly lie very far above us in consciousness, if not so far from us in time as we might first be tempted to suppose. (AM, 246)

Here it seems necessary to distinguish between evolutionary time and the time of common man. We should not measure the increments of evolutionary time against the hours and minutes of our experienced time. Our common time is founded on a constant oscillation, and therefore is relatively unchanging. However, evolutionary time is changing with the speed of evolution, which is constantly and more rapidly accelerating. And due to this acceleration, much more progress is made in evolution during one year in our era than was made in one year one million years ago. With this in mind, the following quotation of Teilhard is to be understood:

> It is certainly not more than one million years since man appeared, isolated and unharmed in one corner of the earth. And this short time has been enough to contain the entire dilating phase of his phyletic development. Now that he is embarking in

Overlooked Aspects of Teilhard's Thought

all his strength on the second major stage of his evolution, why should this phase of accelerated compression last much longer than its predecessor; that is to say, why should it take more than another million years?

Now though at the continually increasing speed at which human affairs are going another million years of hominisation may be startling to the Noosphere, from the astronomical point of view this space of time is quite negligible! (AM, 248)

But Teilhard is speaking of evolutionary years, not of solar years. Besides, account must be taken not only of man's activity, but God's directive influence in the supernatural as well as in the natural order. Though the collective consummation of earthly mankind is a pre-condition of the final, "parousiac" establishment of the Kingdom of God, it is sufficient to bring about neither the parousia nor the Christogenesis which is to precede it. (FM, 237) Both of these lie within the divine power alone. The conclusion, therefore, is that Christogenesis, though perhaps not very far ahead of us in common time, is distant in evolutionary time, due to the progress yet to be made even on a natural level, not to speak of the supernatural level. In this perspective, then, evolutionary time has at least these two applications: (a) it provides a new dynamic concept for Christianity; and (b) it embodies the Will of God, in the sense both of God's directive influence over evolution and His Providence in the supernatural order.

In the concluding paragraph of a summary of the evolutionary thought of Teilhard de Chardin, it is stated:

...it is in his broad general line, his synthesis of the Biblical Hebrew-Christian view of linear time moving towards a climax with the scientist's insight into the innate capacity of matter to complexify, that would seem to provide a richer and more fruitful context for Christianity than did the static, structureless view of history which dominated Western thought during the Middle Ages and for so many years afterwards.[3]

Thus Christianity is understood to be not merely an ancient religion, but the unexpected goal of the development of the whole of evolution, indeed the center and axis of evolution becoming more relevant and important with the passing of evolutionary time.

The second immediate application is seen in an insight of Teilhard written in one of his letters:

> Here is a thought that came to me some time ago about the Will of God: has it occurred to you that it is in some way materialized or even made incarnate, in our inmost depths by *time,* time that carries us along and gives rhythm to our lives, time that passes too slowly or too quickly,...we should acknowledge and love it. (MM, 103)

Furthermore, God gives time a purpose by willing that it manifest His Power in some predestined way. He places creatures in time, and time measures their striving for perfection, their ontological development, and the fulfillment of their purpose. Thus time is a gift which God gives to all men, not only individually, but to the human race as a whole. It provides man with the possibility to make a choice, to answer a challenge, and to cast the die: for or against God, for or against Christ, for or against the attain-

---

[3] J.T. Fraser (ed.), *The Voices of Time.* (New York: Braziller, 1966), p. 76.

ment of the goal for which in the beginning God created the human race.

This goal stands for everything that is good. But the odds against achieving it are increasing daily, even as the hour of choice approaches. Man cannot move forward in genuine progress without God. While he lived, Teilhard set forth the alternatives as clearly as he could, as far as historical development allowed. Approximately a generation later, at a later phase in time, the orientation of his thought well corresponds to the following pronouncement of Pope Paul VI:

> We implore God and beg you, men of our time, to spare yourselves the fateful experience of a Christ-less humanism. A brief reflection on what the history of yesterday and today teaches us would be enough to convince us that human virtues, developed without the Christian charism, can degenerate into their contradictory vices. Man, making himself a giant without a spiritual, Christian animation, collapses under his own weight. He lacks the moral strength which makes him really a man; he lacks the capacity to judge the hierarchy of values; he lacks the transcendental reason which gives lasting motivation and support to his virtues; he lacks, in short, true awareness of himself, of life, of the reasons why of his destinies: man, on his own, does not know who he is. He lacks the authentic prototype of humanity; he creates idols for himself, idols that are fragile and sometimes dishonorable. He lacks the true Son of Man—Son of God: a living model for the true man. True humanism must be Christian. (Christmas message, 1969)

EPILOGUE

"...in the heart of this formless mass You have planted an irrestible and sanctifying urge which makes each one of us cry out 'Lord, make us to be one!'"
(HU, 20)

These essays, though each a unit in itself, have developed a central theme of Teilhard de Chardin: God's immanence in nature, which is directed to the accomplishing of God's transcending purposes through a process of evolution.

According to Teilhard, if a scientist wishes to be true to observable facts, he must admit the "within" as well as the "without" of things. And the Christian, if he wishes to be true to his Faith, must expect to find God at work in nature. As a Christian and a scientist, Teilhard saw God as "within" the universe, and he considered all the world's energy in its various forms as a manifestation of God's power. This is especially true of "radial energy," which reveals itself to man from a study of evolution. For, as Teilhard understands it, "radial energy" is responsible for the evolution of the cosmos towards ever more complex, ever more aware, ever more spiritual things. Basically, it is the real, creative power of God present and working in the whole universe. Taken in this sense, it is not "material" in the usual meaning of the word, and hence in referring to it Teilhard speaks of the "spiritual" power of nature. It is God's gift of Himself (through His continuing act of creation and concurrence) to the universe as a whole; and we have called it the analogue of (something comparable to) *grace* in the supernatural order.

The most primordial manifestation of God's creative power in the universe is "energy" in a more usual meaning, as a "luminous" form—one of the three faces of nature, which Teilhard (together with St. Bonaventure) recognizes as fundamental and common to the whole material universe.

In addition to these verifications of radial energy, in each thing there is a source of energy—a "within" that is identifiable with the intrinsic principle of activity in each thing which Aristotle and St. Thomas Aquinas (in a different context) called the substantial form, or (in man) the rational soul. Another example of radial energy, transferred to a Thomistic context, is the active power (intellectus agens) of the human soul, or the intellect in action. Here, the philosophy of St. Thomas, of the Franciscan School, and of Teilhard find a meeting place. On the one hand, the intrinsic power and action of understanding must be attributed to each man (St. Thomas). However, this does not exclude, but implies, the cooperating, creative, and real effect of God's creative intelligence in the universe (St. Bonaventure's "illumination"). In Teilhard de Chardin, radial energy includes all these factors: God Himself, God's creative power at work in the universe, Man and his power of intelligence, and the actual act of understanding that each man performs. All this is an example of "spiritual" energy as distinct from the material energy of "light," which is God's manifestation of radial energy on a different level. Wherever there is radial energy in one of its forms, there is a corresponding tangential energy on different levels; and it is this energy that is measurable scientifically. However, tangential energy is not completely understandable except in conjunction with radial energy in one of its forms.

Epilogue 129

Modern man cannot afford to take a partial view of reality. Attention is more and more given to the "tangential." The natural sciences are developing on every level. The time has come to recognize fully the importance of radial energy—the spiritual forces at work in the world. Modern man is faced with the challenge to encounter these spiritual forces. Some scientists have foreseen this need. Once when Charles P. Steinmetz was asked what field of research, in his opinion would witness the greatest development in modern times, he replied:

> The greatest discoveries will be along spiritual lines. We scientific men have spent our lives studying physical forces (*Teilhard's tangential energy*), and now—having made the most sensational discoveries in the history of the world—we learn that our knowledge has not brought happiness. Material things will never bring happiness. Scientists must now turn their laboratories over to the study of God, and prayer and the spiritual forces (*Teilhard's radial energy*). Here is the field where miracles are going to occur. Spiritual power is the greatest of the underdeveloped powers, and has the greatest future.

Somewhat in the same spirit, Teilhard once envisioned the day when man's knowledge of God on the natural level would be greatly enhanced by turning attention to the creative power of God in the universe and rising from this knowledge (rather from merely abstractive cognition) to an analogous appreciation of God Himself so manifested. In the words of de Lubac: "After establishing that God must have a personality higher than that which He stimulates, Teilhard envisaged the day when a more profound analysis of the conditions of the evolving universe would lead to a recognizing in the God of Evolution an exact equivalent of the attributes accorded by medieval philosophy to the *Ens a se.*"[1]

With Steinmetz and Teilhard, modern man must admit not only tangential, but *radial* energy. And he must meet it, not only at the level of scientific experiment, but seek to understand as well the higher kinds of "radial" energy which the human reason, the Christian Faith, and even History might reveal. By reason, radial energy can be understood as taking on many different forms (as previously suggested). By Faith, the "within" or "radial" energy at the heart of the universe is known to be the God-Made-Man in Christ. By History, the spiritual forces at work in the world can be seen to be *evil* as well as good; and mankind come of age is called to the "Grand Option" of standing with God revealed in Christ, or of falling with the antichristian forces of evil opposing Him and His purposes in the universe.

In this last connection, Teilhard is far from being a Utopian dreamer and actually calls modern man to the apocalyptic choice between good and evil. "No one," writes Fr. de Lubac, "we must admit, could have been less dazzled by a false Utopian issue, when we remember how quick he was to realize the serious threat contained in the chief form the Utopia of this century takes, the myth of the Golden Age in the future. He pointed out the power it had over men's minds in spite of the weakness of its intellectual basis—and yet, astonishingly, it is this Golden Age that he has been accused of promising." In the context,

---

[1] Lubac, *The Religion of Teilhard, op. cit.,* p. 175. See also p. 89.

de Lubac is insisting that no one can condemn Teilhard for *seeing* that our world is in process of unification and closing-in upon itself at an accelerated rhythm. In the face of this, he does not at all propose a naive optimism. Rather he points to an age of ultimate conflict and of conquest FOR GOD—for those who know how TO SEE!

The creative power of God has led man to his present point in human evolution. With confidence and with decisive resolution, now evolution needs to be consciously directed by men themselves—according to God's purpose. This purpose is known from THE MAN JESUS CHRIST, who, uniting divine and human elements, seeks to draw all things to Himself, by God's creative power, by the intelligent cooperation of men full of faith, and by His triumphant grace.

GLOSSARY OF INTERRELATED TERMS

The reader is referred to the glossary of Teilhard's vocabulary drawn up by Henri de Lubac, *Teilhard Explained* (Paulist Press Deus Books, 1968), pp. 83-89; and to the work of R. Wayne Kraft, *The Relevance of Teilhard* (Fides, Notre Dame, 1968), pp. 152-156.

The purpose of the following glossary is to present some basic concepts of Teilhard as related to other thinkers, especially St. Thomas Aquinas, and to compare Teilhard's viewpoint, in solving the basic philosophical problems, with that of other thinkers.

The Analogy of Being

In St. Thomas, the analogy of being means the basic similarity of all things. Things are similar to each other because each has its own *share* of perfection (the analogy of proportionality) and because each thing (in so far as it is perfect to some degree) is dependent on the One All-Perfect Source, of which it is an imitation (the analogy of attribution). The thought of St. Thomas is primarily concerned here with the *concept* of being, as it finds verification in different orders of reality. For Teilhard, the different verifications of being in the real order lead him not only to the varying (analogous) concept of being, but to the realization that individual beings cannot be understood in isolation and must always be considered as members of a definite order of being and as a manifestation of a definite mode of the divine presence and the divine activity operating manifestly in a given sphere of reality. This is the "divine milieu" or better, "the divine diaphany," by which God appears in and through things, on the different levels of being from the lowest to the highest. In each such order of being, therefore, not only the individuals of that group, but the whole group has a greater share of being, which indicates a clearer manifestation of God present and continually operating in that sphere of dependent being. Thus, cosmogenesis, biogenesis, noogenesis and Christogenesis demonstrate the analogy of being—not taking beings merely as individuals, but as corporate units, which show a similarity to and a dependence on God in different ways in the real order of things. Thus, we can transfer to a metaphysical level, Teilhard's *law of recurrence,* according to which the same property in a series is re-encountered on different levels, intervals and times, allowing for higher synthesis.

Anthropology

Generally, this term is taken in a much more restricted sense than in Teilhard's use of it. For Teilhard, it is the science of man, or mankind, in the widest sense—by means of the natural, social, cultural, moral, philosophical, and theological sciences (de Lubac). In dealing with the question of man, traditional philosophy stresses the spirituality and immortality of the individual man. While in no way underestimating this, Teilhard turns his attention to man *as a species.* He sees man as a culmination of a process, which is still going on, under the divine creative power. In explaining this, Teilhard speaks of *noogenesis, amorization, hominization, personalization, unanimization, pleroma* and *parousia.* Noogenesis is that phase of evolution which began when man first appeared some million years ago (Kraft). It is distinguished from biogenesis in that noogenesis is evolution in the domain of reflective life. Thus, rather than being manifested by the progressive formation of ever more complex biological organisms, it is manifested by the growth of ever more complex and interrelated social institutions which are raising man's awareness of his place in nature (socialization). This process goes on as an effect of the creative energy of God, essentially a force of love tending towards the absolute and personal. This is called amorization, but it in no way implies the denial of counter forces (of evil) also at work in the world. Amorization is akin to hominization, which is the psychosocial evolution of man, described by Kraft as the process whereby mankind's potentialities are more and more fully realized in the world. It is the maturing of mankind, but not in an absolute sense; for account must be taken of the persistence of evil in the world. The peak of hominization according to Teilhard, is to be reached in personalization and unanimization. These last two are the realization of a collective consciousness and of a planetary humanity united in a common effort to promote spiritual progress. They form a part of Christogenesis and are possible, therefore, only through the dominating influence of Christ in the developing of civilization, both in the natural and supernatural orders. The purpose of history will not be achieved until the *pleroma* and the *parousia* (the fulness of Christ's influence in the world and His second coming) have taken place, and thus the crown of all evolution is totally supernatural.

Biogenesis

In Teilhard, biogenesis is another name for biological evolution, which is the evolutionary formation of life and the phenomena contributing to it, including the change from one species to another over extended periods of time. In Teilhard, this process always includes God's creative energy, without which the origin and growth of life would be impossible. Inasmuch as the creative energy of God is in the universe from the beginning and is first manifested by cosmogenesis, biogenesis is conceived as a continuation of the latter. Thus, in Teilhard, individual living things can be considered either as a manifestation of cosmogenesis or of biogenesis. In contrast to this, traditional thinkers tend to consider individual things as separate units, rather than as a collective manifestation of divine power (howsoever designated). In Teilhard, the creature is rarely considered in isolation, but in conjunction with God and His creative energy, as well as a member of a group (to which the individual belongs), which manifests God's presence in a definite way.

Biosphere

Teilhard considers all living things as constituting a *unit,* since they are all united in the creative power of God, the Living Source of all life. In traditional thought, a term like biosphere might be considered as a *mere* figure of speech, whereas for Teilhard this phrase designates an *actual unity* resulting from the divine presence manifested in a special way by the divine creative power in giving life. This unity of all living things is constituted, not merely by the sum total of all living things and their individual relationship to God, but by God's actual and continuing presence to them in a way that is proper to living things (not shared by non-living things). This unity is a *new* manifestation of God in the ontological order, which in Thomistic philosophy must be accounted for by a real relationship, whose point of origin is God Himself and whose effect is the whole group of living creatures considered as a unit.

Christology

Traditional Christology has always centered around the hypostatic union in Christ, which is the union of the divine and human natures in the Person of the Word. Emphasis is given to the implications of this union on the human nature of Christ, viz., on His human sanctity, His human knowledge, and the power of His will. From this results the threefold function of Christ as Priest, Teacher and King, together with the extension of this function to the Mystical Body of Christ, which is His Church, the arc of salvation for the whole world.

Teilhard's Christology takes the hypostatic union as the key to the understanding of the whole cosmos to God. From the very fact of creation, the whole cosmos is united to God in the Word (John, 1). But this union, made manifest in a most perfect way by the Incarnation, is destined to be deepened ever more profoundly until God will be all in all (Paul, I Corinthians 15:28). Through evolution, the creation is an ongoing process, in which God's purpose is gradually achieved, notwithstanding the obstacles of evil and sin. The first and most basic manifestation of God's union with the world is *cosmogenesis,* which is the first phase of evolution, in which matter was formed from energy and assumed ever more perfect forms as time passed on. God is the source of the energy from which the cosmos was and is being created. In this respect God is called the Alpha Point. This union of the whole cosmos with God is common to all the levels of being, but there is a greater union in the realm of life, which is explained by *biogenesis* (q.v.).

Besides cosmogenesis and biogenesis, there occurs an even deeper union with God through *noogenesis,* which is the genesis of reflective thought in the creation of man. Here the Divine Logos manifests His presence in a new and marvellous way, enabling man to participate in His creative intelligence through actual and reflective consciousness. Thus, the Divine Light illumines every man (and all men considered as a group) in accordance with the teaching of St. John (*ibid.*) and of St. Augustine's "illumination," understood as the continuing divine influence inherent to human thought.

Finally, there is Christogenesis, which insures and restores the supernatural destiny of the whole evolutionary process. Just as, in St. Thomas, a natural desire for the beatific (supernatural) vision is not contradictory, so in Teilhard, the supernatural orientation of the whole universe is not repugnant to its natural inclination, though beyond its unaided powers.

The characteristics of Christ's human nature are thus seen as participated by the whole creation in varying degrees: the hypostatic union itself is vaguely reflected in cosmogenesis, Christ's gift of life-giving grace is foreshadowed by biogenesis, Christ's superior knowledge is comparable to noogenesis, and Christ's power of will and sinlessness is the source of Christogenesis.

Because the Divine Word controls the rise of each of the stages of evolution and because in time the Divine Word became Man in Jesus Christ, Christ assumes a cosmic function, by which He directs the evolutionary process to its established destiny. Just as traditional theology stresses the importance of Christ in the supernatural order, Teilhard emphasizes the influence of Christ as Priest, Teacher and King over the whole universe in its natural evolution towards the appointed goal. In some sense, the universe is already holy, as united through the continuing creation (cosmogenesis) with the Divine Word. A portion of the universe (the biosphere) enjoys an even greater contact with God as the Giver of Life. Since Christ holds the creative energy of the universe in His own hands, His continuing influence in these functions parallels His role as Priest in the supernatural order. Christ claims as His own the creative Intelligence, by which mankind continues to progress in thought, and thus His role as Teacher extends over the whole human sphere in the natural order. Finally by His absolute control of the creative energy by which the universe evolves towards its goal, He has absolute control over cosmic events, including man's free acts, directing all towards the one far-off divine event towards which the whole creation moves. Thus, He is universal King in the literal sense of the word. And the Church, which He founded as the phylum of a superior kind of life (grace) when He walked this earth, is the instrument also of the achieving and perfecting of mankind's natural powers over and against all the evil and malice which militates against the divine plan in the world.

Complexity-Consciousness

Teilhard's fundamental law is the law of complexity-consciousness. Under the creative energy of God, matter manifests the property of arranging itself in more and more complex groupings, and at the same time in ever deepening layers of consciousness. At the present stage of evolution, a portion of cosmic matter has become so complex that it has acquired sensible awareness. The most significant portion, man, has even become self-conscious. The law of centrated-complexity-consciousness states that evolutionary progress is understandable by the sequence: energy-matter-life-reflective thought-spirit. Evolutionary progress is to reach its terminal point in the future in Point Omega, or God. However, God has been operative from the beginning as Alpha and Logos. His function as Omega indicates His continuous drawing the universe, in and through man united to Christ, to a conscious realization of its divine destiny of union with Him.

The closest parallel in scholastic thought to the law of complexity-consciousness is perhaps the *hierarchy* of *being,* or the doctrine of *participation,* which states that the relatively perfect things of the universe, which are more or less perfect in relation to each other, derive their perfection because of the definite share that they have in the perfections which are possessed in their fullness by God, the Absolutely Perfect Being. However, here, as in other points of comparison, Teilhard's view is directed, not so much to individuals, but to groups or corporate units seen in evolutionary perspective as progressively achieving a greater degree of participation that brings them closer (not merely in resemblance but in degree of union) to God. This is possible, of course, only because of the creative power of God at work in an evolutionary universe, which consequently displays varying relationships to God.

Glossary of Interrelated Terms 141

Consciousness

In Teilhard, consciousness has a much wider connotation than in traditional thought. It includes (1) "radial force" (energy) or "psychism" in inert matter; (2) simple consciousness of *perception* in animals; (3) reflective consciousness in man (de Lubac). Since God's own creative energy accounts for all these manifestations of His power, even on the lowest level of inert matter, Teilhard detects a "psychism," which is insufficiently known by men at the present time. If explored, with God's help, it could well open the way to the discovery of extraordinary powers in nature and introduce man into the secrets of telepathy, clairvoyance, and other preternatural (if not supernatural) phenomena.

Energy

In Teilhard, energy has a vast extent and varied application of meaning. It can refer not only to physical phenomena, but can be used analogously with an applied meaning to the realm of spirit. Perhaps the closest correspondent in Thomistic language is *ACT*. Just as St. Thomas makes his way from the actions and perfections of the things of this world to their Source, God, or Pure Act, so Teilhard proceeds from the analysis of cosmic matter, understood basically as energy, to the Source of this energy, Who is God. And for Teilhard, the process is not difficult. Energy, as Teilhard finds it in the world, has a "within" and a "without"—an inner and intangible aspect, and a measurable and outward aspect, detectable by sense experience. The first he calls "radial" energy, the second "tangential." The energy usually treated by scientists is "tangential" because tractable. But it is Teilhard's view that the scientist should recognize the mystery of "radial" energy, which is manifested in many forms in conjunction with tangential energy, by which it is revealed to some extent. (Think of the mechanical operation of the human eye contrasted with the fact that it is a "vital" action).

Carrying his argument to the universe as a whole, Teilhard detects a basic "radial energy" or cosmic force behind the evolutionary growth of the universe. This is the creative power of God, or in Thomistic language, the Divine Presence and Concurrence at work in the whole universe, constantly giving existence and cooperating in the activity of the whole universe, and with every individual thing in varying degrees according to the capacity (essence) of each thing. The universe, then, can be seen from two points of view. In one sense, it is something understandable, measurable and, so to say horizontal. On the other hand, it is a manifestation of God Within, Who is beyond human comprehension and possible measurement. Then, each part of the universe also has its measurable and understandable aspects (essential characteristics and accidental relationships), but it also has a vertical and mysterious aspect which is its very existence and its unique relationship to God Who is present to it. It is the task of the Scientist to investigate the former without neglecting the latter, which remains the proper domain of the Philosopher and Theologian. Likewise, the Philosopher and Theologian should relate their *weltanschauung* to the world of nature, which manifests in its own way the same God known by reason and adored in faith.

Finality

Finality is the tendency towards ends which is manifested in the activity even of inorganic matter. The *principle of finality* states that *everything acts for an end.* There is purposefulness in every action. Some good is produced in every action. Action flows upon being, and in acting a being seeks some good as its end.

Here, as in other instances, Teilhard applies a well-known principle in a global fashion. For Teilhard, every tendency towards an end, even on the lowest level, is indicative of the spiritual energy of a Creative Intelligence at work in the universe. In this sense, Teilhard speaks of "psychic temperature." This, according to Kraft, is a figure of speech which expresses the thought that there is a "temperature," analogous to thermal temperature, which measures the intensity or degree of withinness in a clump of matter, or an organism, or a being, or a social institution, or in the whole world.

Furthermore, the principle of finality receives its ultimate application in Teilhard's insistence that the intention of God in creating the universe (the manifestation of His goodness and the salvation of mankind) cannot be frustrated. Thus, he takes "Christogenesis" as the necessary outcome, by the power of God, of the whole of evolution.

A phrase which might sum up these global applications of finality is Teilhard's term, *coherence,* which means that everything in the universe has a common origin and works towards a common goal. We are reminded of St. Paul's phrase: to those who love God, all things work together unto good (Romans 8:28). Another term of Teilhard in this connection is *extrapolation,* which is the means whereby a curve is constructed, with the aid of positive data, beyond what can be observed. Teilhard confidently uses it to preview the future of evolution by reasoning on the unity and coherence of the universe.

The Intuition of Being

The starting point of St. Thomas's philosophy, as interpreted by Maritain, is the *intuition of being.* This is nothing else than the consciousness of reality, of which all men are spontaneously aware. This intuition implies a conscious realization of one's own existence, of the world's existence, and of the objectivity of truth, clearly known in the evident light of the principle of contradiction. Teilhard readily accepted this basic foundation for his own philosophic thought. Building on this knowledge, Teilhard developed his "cosmic sense" which is the perception through the multiplicity of being of the basic unity of the universe. In this sense, we may say that he had a vivid appreciation (by a sort of intuitive or connatural knowledge) of the analogy of being (q.v.) which is for him a "divine diaphany." In and through the changing aspects of beings and of the evolution of the world, Teilhard detects a Common Source (i.e., God) of the creative energy at work in the universe. This vivid realization of Teilhard certainly reveals the mystic orientation of an intuitive soul. Here, rather than with St. Thomas, he seems more linked to the Franciscan School, especially the "contuition of God" of St. Bonaventure.

The One and the Many

In St. Augustine, there is only one immutable Being, God. All others are changeable. St. Thomas explains this through *act* and *potency*. God alone is Pure Act (absolutely perfect). All other things are composites of act and potency, embodying not only their perfections (act) but also their capacities for new ones (potency). In Hegel, all realities are manifestations of the One Idea. Teilhard sees all things (the many), taken both singly and as a whole, in a state of change or development from potency to act. Behind this evolution he discerns the Spiritual Power that both manifests God in some way and accounts for the progress of the universe. This spiritual power, in its origin, is a Divine Person (the Logos) and can be designated by various words (Love, Power, Omega), but in its effects it implies both God's creative energy and all the created manifestations by which God reveals Himself in creation through the progress of evolution. Teilhard's term for this is *cosmogenesis,* which de Lubac defines as follows: the evolutionary formation of the cosmos in space and time and the evolutive phenomena involved.

The Presence of God in Creatures
(or the Presence of Creatures in God)

Traditionally, God is said to be present in creatures *per essentiam, per scientiam, et per potentiam.* This means that God keeps all things in existence, that all things are known to Him, and that all things are subject to His power. This especially refers to each thing individually. Teilhard considers God's presence in the perspective of an evolutionary universe. He speaks of *centration* or *centreity.* De Lubac explains this as the evolutionary process, whereby the "within" of things (their immanence) grows within living and then thinking beings in proportion to the complexification of the "without." Similarly, individual consciousnesses combine to form collective consciousness. There is a supreme center of centration which influences all phenomena—the Omega Point or God. In explaining all this, Teilhard distinguishes various ways and degrees by which God is present to things: by cosmogenesis, biogenesis, noogenesis, and Christogenesis. By these conceptions, Teilhard shifts reference from individual things, taken as individuals, to spheres of reality considered in groups. The *whole* universe (through cosmogenesis) and the whole biosphere (through biogenesis) constantly enjoys God's presence by His creative energy operative in these areas. This corresponds to, and may serve to deepen our understanding of, God's presence *per essentiam.* The whole development of human thought may be considered as a manifestation of (and a greater participation in) God's presence *"per scientiam."* Teilhard calls the development of human thought *noogenesis,* which includes not only God's knowledge of things but His directive influence in the rise of human knowledge over the earth. Finally, the power of God is made manifest by Christogenesis, already begun through the Church in the supernatural order, but destined to occur on a global scale for the accomplishment of God's purpose, notwithstanding human malice. Thus, while in the traditional phrase, *per potentiam,* God is understood to be present through His power in the natural order, Teilhard understands God's power as including both natural and supernatural orders and ordaining one to the other.

Relationship

Perhaps there is no more important concept in St. Thomas than *relationship*. Relationship, taken in its widest meaning, is all-embracing in its significance. Relationship is the *reference* (implication) of one thing to another, or the connection existing between several things or principles, in the real or mental order. In St. Thomas, it is the relationship of all things to God that constitutes the order of the universe. The unity, truth, and goodness of things find their source in the Nature, Mind and Will of God. The distinctiveness of each thing is rooted in its unique relationship to God. In the case of a human person, this unique relationship, involving an intellectual, free and spiritual nature similar to God's, makes one capable of entering into union with the Person of God. The whole material universe is a vast network of real, accidental relationships without which the universe could not be understood.

Perhaps, it is in terms of relationship that Teilhard's world view can be best explained to a Thomist. The unity of the universe, with its real and necessary relationship to God, is something very real to Teilhard. He speaks of the "divine diaphany," inviting us (1) to understand God in His manifestation through the *whole* universe as well as through individual things; (2) to grasp the varying levels of reality as necessarily revealing distinct levels of relationships to God, Who is present to them, not merely individually but as groups, as cause of these relationships; (3) to penetrate the effect-cause relationships on the varying levels of the evolving cosmos as a dynamic process open to intelligent observation and analysis. As a result of this, Teilhard concludes that (1) the universe is truly one (not, however, in a pantheistic sense); (2) the "multiple," which was the first condition of the stuff of the universe, is slowly unified by evolution, which is nothing else than the *relating* of the universe in varying stages to God in ever deeper fashion;

(3) in this whole process, a "Center" of all the relationships involved is necessary, and this Center is God Himself, the Omega Point, Who revealed Himself in history in the Person of Jesus of Nazareth. Thus, Teilhard discerns and proclaims the implementation of the biblical "restoration of all things in Christ," through a genuine historical process, with natural and supernatural means, notwithstanding the obstacle of sin, both as known through human experience (personal sin) and through revelation (original sin).

Substance-Accident

In traditional philosophy, a substance is something capable of existing in itself. An accident is something capable of existing in another. Allied to those concepts are *substantial* and *accidental,* the former meaning the necessary and relatively stable, the latter the unnecessary and changing aspects of reality. Following the lead of modern scientists, Teilhard does not generally use the terms, substance and accidents. In a larger context, he prefers to speak of the "within" and the "without" of things. The "within" is the inner, intangible aspect of all things, beings and institutions. The "without" is that aspect of all things, beings and institutions which is detectible by sense experience. Using this terminology in a flexible way, Teilhard never isolates one from the other, the "without" always presupposing as its counterpart a "within." This is similar to the scholastic idea that accidents are the manifestations of substance, which they presuppose.

The World Stuff

The stuff of the universe is initial energy—still undifferentiated—from which the world is made, possessing a "within" and a "without," a material and a spiritual aspect (de Lubac). In this respect, Teilhard's thought seems to approach the "metaphysics of light" of the Franciscan School. For the basic constituent of the universe seems to be light energy, which is interconvertible with mass or matter according to the famous equation $E=mc^2$. The first is the "within," which he calls "radial" energy, and the second is the "without," which he calls "tangential." It is the latter which is associated with the tangible reality of the cosmos. All phenomena, which can be measured in terms of tangential energy, involve a "within" which, though not subject to direct, sensible observation and measurement, must be recognized by the mind. The "within" is therefore the "intelligible" or "spiritual" aspect of things. Besides the sum total of all measurable energy of the universe and which is subject to the law of entropy, Teilhard suggests that there is a spiritual kind of energy in the universe (the creative power of God in constant operation towards higher forms of life). Hence the universe, taken as a whole, is not merely to be considered as a physical and material whole, which is measurable, but as a manifestation of cosmic energy (or creative power) of God, Who gives it its unity, coherence and destiny.

World View (Weltanschauung)

The *weltanschauung* of a thinker is his integrated view of the world. Just as St. Thomas integrated the philosophic world outlook, which was gaining acceptance in his time, to divine revelation, so Teilhard sought to interpret commonly accepted views of the contemporary scientific mentality with Faith. Scientifically, the world has been making progress, notwithstanding an appalling increase of moral evil in the world. Who controls this scientific progress, and where is it leading? For Teilhard, there is only one answer: the source of the cosmic energy at work in the universe is no other than Christ, the God-Man, Who is destined to subject all things to Himself. By the "breath of his mouth and the brightness of his coming" (Thessalonians 2:8), and through the cooperation of those who know God's plan for the world, the universe must be sanctified and rendered worthy of a glorified Christ and a glorified humanity. This is the "good news" for a century globally tormented by wars, violence, persecution and hate. *Oportet illum regnare!* (I Corinthians 15:25) Christ must reign. God "has let us know the mystery of his purpose, the hidden plan He so kindly made in Christ from the beginning to act upon when the times had run their course to the end: that He would bring everything together under Christ, as head, everything in the heavens and everything on earth." (Ephesians 1:9-10)

SELECTED INDEX

(of terms explained in the preceding glossary)

The Analogy of Being 133
Anthropology. 134
Biogenesis 136
Biosphere 136
Christology. 137
Complexity-Consciousness 139
Consciousness. 141
Energy 141
Finality. 143
The Intuition of Being 144
The One and the Many. 144
The Presence of God in Creatures. 145
Relationship. 146
Substance-Accident 148
The World Stuff. 148
World View (Weltanschauung). 149